An
Economist
Walks
into
a Brothel

An Economist Walks into a Brothel

*And Other Unexpected Places
to Understand Risk*

ALLISON SCHRAGER

PORTFOLIO/PENGUIN

Portfolio/Penguin
An imprint of Penguin Random House LLC
penguinrandomhouse.com

Most Portfolio books are available at a discount when purchased in quantity for sales promotions or corporate use. Special editions, which include personalized covers, excerpts, and corporate imprints, can be created when purchased in large quantities. For more information, please call (212) 572-2232 or e-mail specialmarkets@penguinrandomhouse.com. Your local bookstore can also assist with discounted bulk purchases using the Penguin Random House corporate Business-to-Business program. For assistance in locating a participating retailer, e-mail B2B@penguinrandomhouse.com.

ISBN 9780525533962 (hardcover)
ISBN 9780525533979 (ebook)
ISBN 9780525542827 (international edition)

Printed in the United States of America
1   3   5   7   9   10   8   6   4   2

BOOK DESIGN BY AMANDA DEWEY

Penguin is committed to publishing works of quality and integrity. In that spirit, we are proud to offer this book to our readers; however, the story, the experiences, and the words are the author's alone.

While the author has made every effort to provide accurate internet addresses and other contact information at the time of publication, neither the publisher nor the author assumes any responsibility for errors or for changes that occur after publication. Further, the publisher does not have any control over and does not assume any responsibility for author or third-party websites or their content.

Contents

CONTENTS

CONTENTS

CONTENTS

CONTENTS

An
Economist
Walks
into
a Brothel

Chapter 1

INTRODUCING RISK:
The What and Unusual Where of It

The revolutionary idea that defines the boundary between modern times and the past is the mastery of risk: the notion that the future is more than a whim of the gods and that men and women are not passive before nature.

—PETER BERNSTEIN, *AGAINST THE GODS*

Despite the bright Nevada sun, the room was dark and the air stuffy; an obscure *I Love Lucy* rerun played on mute. A bell rang and a nondescript, pudgy man entered. Suddenly about a dozen women came running from a maze of long hallways, whooshed past me, and lined up in the foyer. Each woman folded her hands behind her back, stepped forward, and said her name. The man pointed to the second woman on the left, a zaftig platinum blonde wearing a red thong and lace bra. She took his hand and led him to her room.

Welcome to the Moonlite BunnyRanch. A legal brothel is perhaps not where you would expect to find an economist who specializes in retirement finance, but I'm an unusual kind of risk junkie. I hunt risk to understand it better. I don't seek out adrenaline-charged situations. I've never bungee jumped, I don't ski, and I may be the only New Yorker who is afraid to jaywalk. Rather than look for risky situations for the rush of defying the odds, I search for unusual places that can teach me more about risk and how to manage it.

I was trained to shape policy, advise captains of industry, or write research papers at a university. And yet there I was, sitting on a red velvet sofa in a vinyl-sided house in a remote corner of Nevada because unusual markets like sex work thrive on risk. We can always find better ways to measure and reduce risk, so I go wherever people might be defying the odds. After all, financing retirement when you don't know if the stock market will soar or crash, or how long you will live, requires mastering risk.

Sex work is a risky business. I went to Nevada to understand how the industry isolates and assigns a price to this risk. Most sex workers and their clients could be arrested or subject to violence. Sex workers who find their customers on the streets are thirteen times more likely to be murdered than the general population. Thirty-five percent of sex-worker homicides are committed by serial killers. Paying for or selling sex carries a stigma: sex workers and their customers face social, professional, and legal repercussions if they are caught. I went to the brothel to understand what it costs to eliminate this risk.

WHAT IS RISK?

When people hear the word "risk," they automatically think of something terrible, the worst-case scenario, like losing their job, their wealth, or their spouse.

But we need to take risks to make our lives better. We must gamble to get what we want, even if it comes with the possibility of loss. If we want a great relationship, we risk heartbreak. If we want to get ahead at work, we have to volunteer for projects that we might fail at. If we avoid risk, our lives won't move forward. Technically, risk describes everything that might happen—both good and bad—and how probable each of these outcomes is.

Even the history of the word "risk" illustrates our complicated feelings about the concept: it derives from *rhizikón*, an ancient Greek seafaring term that describes a dangerous hazard. Though its usage evolved slightly over the years, it always described something perilous. But the meaning changed in the sixteenth century, when exploration of the New World began, and people started to think about risk as something controllable—not left to fate. The Middle High German word *rysigo* means "to dare, to undertake, enterprise, hope for economic success."

Whether you realize it or not, you take risks large and small, every day, in all parts of your life. The good news is that you don't have to leave it all up to chance and hope for the best. This book will show you how to mindfully take a risk *and* minimize the possibility that the worst will happen.

We are often taught to think of decisions in terms of "if I do X, then I'll get Y," but in reality any time we make a decision, a range of Ys could happen, from a superior Y to a terrible outcome. Once we recognize this, we can take steps to alter the range of Ys. We can't guarantee a positive outcome, but when we think about risk more strategically we can increase the odds that things will work out. This is sometimes called taking a calculated risk, but there is a science to risk that helps you understand what is worth trying and how to maximize the chance of success when you do take a risk.

The science of risk I'm referring to comes from financial economics. While you might be imagining men with slicked-back hair and fancy suits trying to make money—or take yours—most of what goes on in financial markets is simply buying and selling risk. Risk in finance is an estimate of everything that might happen to an asset—say, the odds of a stock going up 2 percent or 20 percent, or dropping 60 percent. Once risk is measured it can be bought or sold: people can choose to increase risk or reduce it, according to their preference. Financial economics studies risk in financial markets, but its lessons can be applied to any market or decision we encounter in our lives.

For example, like any risk scholar, I would never take a New York City crosstown bus, because travel time is totally unpredictable: it takes thirty minutes on average to cross the island of Manhattan via bus, but commutes of more than an hour or as short as fifteen minutes are possible, depending on the day or time. If I walk, it takes thirty-five minutes—every time. When I walk, I don't have to worry about excessive traffic or lots of stops to let people on and off the bus. Walking crosstown is almost perfectly predictable, and for me takes just about as long as riding the bus. To put it in terms of financial economics: if you need to decide between two portfolios with similar returns, choose the one that is less risky.

These lessons from financial economics can be useful whenever we need to make a risky decision, but most of us never learn them. I have a PhD in economics, but I didn't learn much about finance until I finished graduate school. I had assumed financial economics was simply the study of how people try to beat the stock market to get rich. While that's part of it, because increasing risk offers the possibility of making more money, financial economics is more than that: it is the study of risk.

As I learned more about financial economics, I started to see how its market-based lessons on risk could translate into a new way to understand and see the wider world. Knowing how to use these tools would empower us to make better complex risky decisions every day, from deciding to go back to school or take a job at a start-up, to allocating an amount of time to work on a project or determining how much to bid on a dream house.

The economics of risk are everywhere. When writing this book, I did something economists rarely do. Rather than sit at my desk at home and just look at data, I spent many hours in the company of non-economists, far from Wall Street, and asked them how they manage risk in their lives and careers.

Everyone I interviewed has found clever ways to identify and manage risk in a rapidly changing economy. Their stories illustrate the most important principles of financial economics better than any story about the stock market ever could.

BROTHEL-NOMICS

The owner of the Moonlite BunnyRanch when I visited was Dennis Hof, a large, slightly hunched, bald man in his seventies who had an imposing presence. He often wore a bowling shirt and khaki pants and walked the halls of the brothel flanked by young blondes vying for his attention and approval. Hof died in October 2018 at the age of seventy-two, found in his luxury suite at one of the brothels by porn star Ron Jeremy.

Hof grew up a beloved only child in Arizona. In high school he worked at a gas station, knocked up his girlfriend, and married her. Soon after, Hof started buying gas stations; he sold gas illegally during the 1970s energy crisis and pocketed a small fortune. He had a series of affairs and his marriage fell apart. Hof moved to San Diego, started a business selling time-shares, and befriended people in the porn industry. He also became a regular customer at Nevada's legal brothels.

The only places in the United States where selling sex is lawful are a handful of counties in Nevada, where the industry is heavily regulated. Licit sex workers must work out of a licensed brothel, be regularly screened for sexually transmitted diseases, and undergo extensive background checks.

In the 1980s, when Hof and his friends frequented the brothels, they were dingy, sad places—often a trailer in the desert where women were expected to perform any sex act the customer wanted for whatever price the house set. The women weren't allowed to leave for days at a time.

In 1993, Hof bought the Moonlite brothel in a small town just outside Carson City and decided to approach sex work the same way he sold time-shares. He abolished set prices and let the women choose what services they wanted to provide and to whom. He set up the business so every woman at the brothel worked as an independent contractor who could come and go as she pleased* and negotiate the terms of each transaction herself. This gave her more autonomy and an incentive to hustle and ask for more money. By the time he died, Hof had bought six other brothels in Nevada; I visited four of them.

In many ways, the brothel is like any other workplace. There are weekly staff meetings (in a departure from the tradition at most companies, the women often wear outlandish hats and drink tea), access to financial advisers, performance bonuses, and even corporate housing (Hof owned a local apartment building where many of the staff live). The Moonlite BunnyRanch, his best-known brothel, was even featured in a racy reality TV show called *Cathouse*.

But where Hof provided value was by reducing risk, for both buyers and sellers of sex.

Supply

During my time in Nevada, I met dozens of sex workers, and each one does the work for a different reason. Some of the stories are heartbreaking; others simply describe a woman who likes her job and the money it provides. I met women with MBAs and PhDs. And in all my years studying economics and finance, I've never met a shrewder businessperson than Shelby Starr.

Starr was one of the top earners in Hof's seven brothels.† She is in her

---

* She must be at the brothel during her assigned shifts.
† Starr now works at the Mustang Ranch, another legal brothel outside of the Hof network.

midforties, curvaceous, with flowing blonde hair, and speaks in a warm, raspy Texas accent. Starr is married with three children, and except for her unusual career, she lives a typical life. She works all day at the brothel and comes home to her family most nights. We met in Starr's bedroom to talk about her business.

Before starting at the brothel, Starr lived a double life: marketing executive by day and exotic dancer on the side. Or it might be more accurate to say that she was a high-paid exotic dancer "on the conference circuit" who had a corporate job on the side. "There's a conference circuit for strippers?" I asked.

There isn't an *official* circuit, Starr explained, but she noticed that she earned more dancing when certain conferences were in town. She researched the locations of different conferences—tech paid best—and built relationships with strip clubs all over the country so she could follow the most lucrative events to different cities.

Not surprisingly, Starr earned more by dancing than at her corporate gig. She admitted that she only kept her day job to avoid the stigma associated with being an exotic dancer, in part because she comes from a religious family. A traditional job also made it easier to live in a small community and raise children. For more than fifteen years she quietly pursued both careers. But Starr acknowledged that her corporate/ *Flashdance* lifestyle "was pretty obvious. I mean, with the platinum hair, fake tan, and boobs, I wasn't fooling anyone."

By the time she reached her late thirties, Starr felt she was getting too old to keep dancing. She hated her corporate position, and the company wanted her to relocate; then her husband lost his job. It was time to try something new. Starr had heard that legal sex work paid well and she was familiar with the BunnyRanch from the reality show, so she contacted the brothel manager, Madam Suzette. Starr was invited to come to Nevada, at her own expense, for a two-week trial.

That first trip is a major gamble, and making it is one of the biggest risks the women in the brothel face. They must pay their own way, outfit themselves in the right clothes and makeup, obtain a license, and undergo a thorough health check. These up-front costs can run about $1,500, a small fortune for most of the women, who are often young and working at low-paid jobs for employers who would sooner fire them than grant a two-week sabbatical. And once they obtain a license to be a legal sex worker, that fact would be revealed on subsequent background checks, no matter how short-term the gig.

Add to these concerns the chance that they wouldn't even get the job and earn back their money, or that the brothel wouldn't be a good fit. Starr was worried about the dynamics of the house, with so many women cooped up together, all vying for the same clients. But the potential upside was huge: an opportunity to make more money than ever before.

Starr had a great first two weeks. She promptly packed up her family and moved them to Nevada. Now the sole breadwinner, she grosses more than $600,000 a year. She is fully "out" to everyone about her lifestyle, even her children.

But it all comes at a cost. How much of her earnings is Starr willing to pay to the brothel for the opportunity to sell sex legally? Ten percent? Twenty-five?

I was floored to find out that Starr hands over *half* of her earnings to the brothel. Why? The main reason is to reduce the risk involved with sex work. But that's not brothel workers' only expense; they must also cover travel to Nevada,* a fee to use the bedrooms, doctor bills for disease screenings, clothes, makeup, condoms, and sex toys. As independent contractors, the women have to pay taxes on all their earnings, which accounts for 30–40 percent of their remaining pay. No wonder several of them proudly told me they could write off sex toys and pornography as tax deductions.

I surveyed twenty-three women about their last five clients, or all the recent clients they could remember, at four different Hof-owned

---

* They may live in other parts of the country.

brothels, analyzing 110 transactions.* The average hourly rate is $1,400, though fees can vary significantly depending on the provider and scope of the service. Rates range from a low of $360 an hour (charged by a woman who is new to the brothel) to a high of $12,000 an hour.

For that much money, wouldn't the women be tempted to work illegally and keep it all? Most sex workers do. The Internet transformed the illegal side of the business: sex workers don't have to hand over their earnings to an agency or a pimp anymore because they can advertise online and market themselves directly to a wide range of clients. But the going rate for illegal sex is much lower than $1,400 an hour.

I was able to estimate the price of illegal sex using four years' worth of data (2013 to 2017) scraped from the website of the *Erotic Review,* a publication that offers detailed reviews of sex-work transactions.† Across U.S. cities, and in northern Nevada, the average going rate for high-end escorts is $350 an hour. Prices are a little higher in big cities like New York and Las Vegas, about $400 an hour.

The 300 percent markup for legal services surprised me.‡

But that $1,400 an hour a legal sex worker earns isn't as much of a windfall as it seems to be when you tally up costs: 50 percent to the house, 30–40 percent to the taxman, not to mention fixed expenses for clothing, health care, and tools of the trade. Take-home hourly pay is similar to, and sometimes less than, that of illegal workers, and that doesn't even include outlays for travel and relocation to Nevada or having to deal with the politics and structure of the brothel. From

---

* A few of the women I interviewed had worked at brothels outside the Hof network and claimed the prices were similar.

† The data includes three hundred thousand observations on different sex transactions, including sex act performed, length of time, and cost.

‡ Is there a premium attached to working with a pimp? In 2003, the economist Steven Levitt and the sociologist Sudhir Venkatesh estimated that prostitutes who work with pimps earn about 50 percent more than those who work independently. They surmised that the markup derived from a pimp's ability to find more clients than a streetwalker could find on her own, but their research predated the move to online advertising. In the age of the Internet and social media, a pimp's ability to find customers adds less value. According to the *Erotic Review* data, high-end escorts who advertise online earn a similar amount whether or not they are affiliated with an agency.

an economic perspective, leaving the brothel seems to be the better choice.

When I asked the women whether they ever thought about striking out on their own, a few mentioned that they were tempted at times and that anyone who said otherwise was lying. But each woman said there was no way she would do it and gave the same reason, in Starr's words: "It is just too risky. I know I am safe here."

The women who work in the brothels don't need to worry about whether their clients are homicidal lunatics or undercover cops. I spoke to several who had worked illegally on their own, and all had had at least one bad experience.

The brothel employs security guards, and each room has a panic button. The women told me how a few customers crossed the line by asking too many questions about their personal lives and finding out their real names and addresses. Hof's brothels have a zero-tolerance policy for such behavior: these clients are banned from the brothel and security guards follow the women home.

Legal brothels offer something women can't get on their own: safety in exchange for earnings. Brothel work is what is known in finance as a hedge: giving up some of your potential earnings in exchange for reducing risk. The hefty price of this hedge tells you how much risk reduction is worth to sex workers in Nevada. The price of a sexual encounter can also tell you how much extra money sex workers need to take more risk. Economists have estimated that sex workers in Mexico charge 23 percent more to customers who won't use a condom. The economists believe that 23 percent represents compensation for the additional risk.

Demand

It is even more surprising that customers will pay three times the illegal price to come to the brothel.

In any illicit market—exotic animals, guns, sex, stolen IDs—what determines if an illegal good costs more or less than the legal alternative is who has more market power, the buyer or the seller. Power usually comes down to availability. Take cigarettes: You can buy them legally at drugstores and gas stations, so you would only buy them on the black market if you got a really big discount. You would not assume the risks of an illegal transaction (being arrested or fined, for instance) unless you stood to save a lot of money. This isn't the case for most illegal markets, however: the seller charges a markup because she is hawking something that's either hard to find (exotic animals or obscure currencies) or restricted (guns, sex, or drugs) in the mainstream market.

I assumed legal sex work would follow the more obscure illegal-market scenario. It is hard to buy and available only in remote corners of Nevada, which takes hours of flying and driving for most Americans. In contrast, illegal sex is comparatively easier to buy, available online in almost every city. For convenience alone, you would think illegal sex workers could charge more. But illegal sex is a risky purchase and customers are willing to pay to reduce that risk.

Another good example of how risk drives demand is the most popular and expensive service, called the Girlfriend Experience, or GFE in brothel-speak. It involves the pleasantries of a typical relationship: kissing, cuddling, talking, going to dinner or the movies. GFE is offered in the illegal market as well, where it also commands a premium over standard sex.

Men pay more for the service because it offers the ultimate risk-free encounter: the illusion of intimacy free from the risk of rejection or the demands of commitment. This explains why the brothel's biggest earners aren't nineteen-year-olds who appear in pornographic magazines but middle-aged women like Starr who offer comfort and intimacy. The older workers' advanced people skills give them an advantage when it comes to cultivating clients, meeting their needs, and making them feel safe and comfortable. "Most of the guys are just lonely," one of the women remarked. "Many of them don't even want to have sex."

Patrons of the BunnyRanch know that the typical risks associated with paying for sex and even regular dating are absent here. The brothel tries to take risk out of the equation at every possible step. If a customer pays with his credit card, the charge appears on his statement under a harmless-sounding name. The buyer values the safety of legal sex work so much that he's willing to travel and pay a large premium; this in turn gives legal brothels market power and the ability to impose big markups for their services.

Hof described to me the customer experience he aimed to provide: "You don't have to worry you'll get arrested and it will get back to your wife, or the girl will blackmail you; you don't have to worry about getting a disease because all the ladies are tested each week."

Unlike traditional pimps, Hof didn't get rich by forcing young women into dangerous situations. Just the opposite: He made his money by enabling a safe transaction between a sex worker and her client. Each of them was willing to pay for that safety. That was where Hof took his cut.

FINANCE: THE SCIENCE OF RISK

A 50 percent cut is what sex workers pay to eliminate their risk. Sex customers pay a 300 percent markup. Is this too much or too little? You decide. The market for sex is an extreme example, one in which most of us will never participate. That markup reflects the price the market has assigned to risky sex. Unusual markets often provide the clearest insight into how risk is assessed, bought, and sold. Because nothing is hidden in markets like sex work, the subtleties that exist in all markets are made obvious. This is why we can learn the most by studying how business is conducted at the edges of the economy and apply that knowledge to more typical economic transactions.

Think about how often we are given the option to pay to reduce risk: we are offered an extended warranty on a new appliance, we are offered different fare classes on a flight that increase the odds of getting space in the overhead compartment, or we are offered the variable or fixed interest rate on a loan. In each situation, we either give up something to reduce risk or take a gamble so we can get more for less. In the brothel, the price of risk is front and center: both sex workers and customers know exactly what they are paying for. In more everyday transactions, the price of risk may be hidden in the fine print or bundled with other services.

Financial science aims to separate out what portion of a price is driven by risk. Once that price is clear, it becomes much easier to identify the risks we face and figure out the best ways to take and reduce risk. Each chapter of this book will help you gain deeper insight into how risk can be valued, enhanced, or reduced by exploring different markets through the lens of financial economics. This offers a framework to understand the role risk plays in unusual, disparate markets.

In most areas of economics, value is based on scarcity. It doesn't work quite the same way in financial economics. Financial economics assumes risk is also a critical component of value. Goods that lessen risk tend to cost more. This critical piece of information can revolutionize the way you assess everyday decisions and help you make better, more informed choices.

Let's examine how this principle plays out in the pricing of airline fares. You may not realize it, but when you buy the cheapest ticket, you are at the top of the list to be bumped if the airline oversells the flight—check out the fine print. A cheap ticket comes with the risk of being forced to miss your flight. Purchasing a more expensive ticket reduces that risk.

Making a good risky decision requires transparency and spotting what you are paying for risk. In a poorly functioning market, we cannot make this distinction. For example, prices are not transparent in underground markets like criminal enterprises (think of illegal sex work before the Internet), so risk cannot be rationed based on price. Price opacity is why sex work traditionally had a flawed risk allocation; pimps took most of the money and almost none of the risk. Crime is an extreme example, but when prices are not clear it's more common for us to overpay or take on more risk than we realize—remember, the cheaper the airline ticket, the higher the odds of getting bumped for that discount.

Some markets do not reward risk in a sensible way, usually because something interferes with its proper functioning; for example, information is scarce, risk is hard to measure, or something limits competition among buyers or sellers of risk. In later chapters I will explain how an impaired risk market is behind all those bad movies made in Hollywood (chapter 4) and slower racehorses (chapter 8).

When we're able to isolate risk in a transaction and determine how it is valued, we can make better decisions. Finance uses many technical tools to identify, price, and sell risk, but the basic ideas behind them are easy to understand and apply to any market or problem. Once you master these tools, you'll never again hesitate when choosing a restaurant, a health insurance plan, or an extended warranty.

THE RULES OF RISK

Policymakers, journalists, and academics often complain about people's inability to understand risk. We are in fact prone to behaviors that cause us to distort the risks we face, and because of this we sometimes make choices that aren't in our best interest. But that doesn't mean we aren't capable of understanding risk and formulating clever strategies to manage it. You probably already have a few up your sleeve, such as a surefire strategy to get to the airport on time or a knack for picking a new restaurant everyone in your family will like. Most people make smart, sophisticated risky decisions in one area of their life but don't apply the same thinking to another—like retirement planning. We all have the potential to be great risk strategists, but few of us are taught how to practice risk analysis in our decision making.

Once you learn a few key principles behind financial economics, what makes one risky decision easier than another becomes clearer and you can apply your best risk strategies to every area of your life.

This book walks you through the following five rules for better assessing and employing risk in your life. Each one describes a different risk concept from financial economics, illustrated through people and places testing its limits, and then shows you how to apply this concept in your everyday life.

1. No risk, no reward.

Risking loss is the price we pay for the chance of getting more. But there are ways to maximize your chance of success. This book will explain different sophisticated strategies from financial economics, but the single most effective way to increase the odds that risk taking will pay off is fairly simple: define what risk and reward mean to you. The biggest mistake people make when they take a risk is not having a well-defined goal. It sounds so simple, but we often take big risks without thinking through what we want, just that we need a change and want to shake things up. But a risk without a well-defined reward rarely goes well. Knowing what we want can be hard, but I'll show you a strategy to identify and define reward and then gauge how much risk to take in any risky decision. It may seem counterintuitive, but the best way to define a risky reward is to start by defining the opposite of risk, whatever is risk-free.

We will then discover how to measure risk. People often measure risk based on what has happened in the past, but does the past tell us anything about the future, and if so, what history is most relevant? Even if the past is a useful guide, what events in the past are most likely to happen again? I will explain how we can make sense of our past to gauge the risks we take today.

Finally, we'll discuss the different types of risk we all face and how to spot the difference between one-offs that are usually easy to manage and system-wide events that are harder to deal with.

2. I am irrational and I know it.

We don't always behave the way economic and financial models predict when faced with a risky decision. We have an aversion to loss and sometimes this can lead us to take bigger risks than we should or even realize. Better awareness is key, and I will show you how to stay rational even when the stakes are high.

How we perceive risk is often not based on objective probabilities; rather, it depends on how risk is presented to us. We sometimes assume certainty when there is none, or that something unlikely is probable. I will help you change how you perceive risk no matter how it's presented to you, to keep you in control.

3. Get the biggest bang for your risk buck.

The bigger the potential reward, the more risk you must take. But a bigger risk doesn't always mean more reward. Sometimes we face two options that offer the possibility for the same expected reward, but one is riskier than the other. Taking more risk than necessary is inefficient. You will learn how to diversify to reduce unnecessary risk and keep your potential for more reward intact.

4. Be the master of your domain.

Next we'll dive into risk management, or how to increase the odds of getting more and reduce the odds of getting less. Once you've eliminated unnecessary risk, you can still further reduce the remaining risk.

One strategy to minimize risk is hedging. Hedging protects you from losing by a counterbalancing action, trying to strike a balance between risk and safety, like the women in the brothel do. Or, hedging might be taking two bets at the same time where one pays off when the other does not. The result is you give up some potential gains to reduce the potential for loss.

The other method to reduce risk is insurance, where you pay someone else to bear downside risk for you. Unlike hedging, after you pay for insurance, you keep all the potential upside.

Risk management reduces the odds the worst will happen, but it also creates a new downside. Any tool that reduces risk can also be used to enhance it; a safety net can either catch you when you fall or be used as a slingshot to catapult you higher. The same is true for hedging and insurance. Not only that, reducing risk can embolden more risk taking and result in using extra leverage to take even bigger risks.

5. Uncertainty happens.

Even the best risk assessment can't account for everything that might happen. Risk estimates everything we think might happen, but there are also all the things we never imagined could happen— the difference between risk (what can be estimated) and uncertainty (the things we never anticipate). Things you don't expect always come up, and you can prepare for the unexpected. We'll review how to protect yourself from uncertainty.

THE WORLD GETS RISKIER AND YOU CAN OWN IT

From a risk perspective, there has never been a better time to be alive. For most of human history we regularly faced truly catastrophic risks like famines and plagues. Take an easy decision that most of us wouldn't think twice about today, like going to visit a friend in a different city. In the past, you might have exposed yourself and your family to a horrible, deadly disease by taking that trip. These days, if you live in a rich, stable country, those risks are highly unlikely.

But our modern selves face more acute risks that threaten our way of life. With the economy going through a major transition, no one's job seems as safe and certain as it once did. Until recently, our employers absorbed most of the risk we faced, taking on retirement risk by offering us pensions. They sheltered us from wage risk and offered job stability, with a steady paycheck and regular, predictable hours. These benefits are increasingly rare in the twenty-first century.

To help us, we have more tools than ever before generated by data and algorithms that can be used to both measure and mitigate risk. More data offers the potential to measure risk more accurately, and technology helps us interpret that data in seconds to be able to make quick decisions. Often, we can do this from our phones: Waze minimizes the risk of being stuck in traffic; Netflix increases the odds of watching a movie you'll love; travel websites can predict whether the price of a flight will go up or down. Data and technology may raise the stakes in our economy, but they also deliver once esoteric and inaccessible risk estimates to the masses.

As we've seen from the big busts in the finance industry, the tools of financial economics can be useless, sometimes even harmful, without some knowledge of how to use them. That's true for large and small risks we face. Google Maps may offer an estimate that it will take fifteen minutes to get to work today, but as you know all too well, that is a very rough estimate. Google would be more accurate to tell you fifteen minutes plus or minus five minutes, depending on traffic conditions. The five minutes is a risk estimate.* If you don't account for that extra time, you might be late.

If used correctly, the tools derived from financial economics help us understand trade-offs and hazards that might lie ahead. They can help us make better choices and reduce risk. Financial models provide a road map for the decisions we face in life. If you plan a trip using a map, you have a route for how to get to your destination and where it lies relative to other places. Having that map increases the odds you reach your destination, and it might make you more inclined to get on the road and take a trip.

But using a road map doesn't guarantee a safe journey. The map probably doesn't include the tree you might smash into because you were texting while driving. It also doesn't include the Mack truck that might accidentally slam into you even if you drive safely.

But that does not mean you should throw out the map. It still increases the odds of a successful journey, especially if you've been taught how to read a map. In the following chapters, I'll share stories of risk takers from diverse corners of the economy, from sex workers and soldiers to surfers and horse breeders. The one thing they all have in common is risk. None of these people have ever worked on Wall Street, but they use the same strategies financiers use to manage risk. Their stories illustrate how the lessons of finance can help us all navigate the modern economy.

---

* Google has this data but doesn't make it public.

RULE 1

NO RISK, NO REWARD

We won't stay in Nevada for this rule, though often when people hear "no risk, no reward," they automatically think of high stakes in Vegas. This powerful but often misunderstood statement is where most people go wrong. They focus on the risk part, just thinking of all the risks they face when making a decision. But really, the most important part is reward. A risk is more likely to work out if you are seeking a reward you actually want. It sounds so obvious, but we often take risks just because we want change. And when we do that, we often lose, no matter what happens.

This rule teaches you to know where you're going before jumping in the risk fast lane. Chapter 2 explains how identifying the well-defined reward you're seeking increases the odds of a risk working. And often we need to define reward in terms of what risk isn't—or what is risk-free. "Risk-free" is one of the most powerful concepts in finance. Chapter 3 explains how to use risk-free as the foundation of financial decision making.

Chapter 4 explores how to measure risk, and how to know what risks you should worry about. Then, in chapter 5, we'll examine the different types of risk we face. Some risks are easier to deal with than others, and it pays to know the difference.

Chapter 2

REWARD:
Getting What You Want Takes Knowing What You Want

*If you don't know where you are going,
you might wind up someplace else.*

—YOGI BERRA

Taking a risk without a goal is just like getting in a car and driving around aimlessly expecting to wind up in a great place. You might land somewhere wonderful, but odds are you'll end up somewhere you don't want to be.

We all have days when we want to quit our jobs, ditch our relationships, and start fresh. Most of us know people who've done this, and more often than not, the gamble did not pay off. They still faced the same job and relationship issues they did before. In order to have a better job, we need to know what we want from our career. In order to have a better relationship, we need to be clear about what we are looking for in a partner.

Obviously, if you have a destination in mind, you are much more likely to end up there. Yet we often take risks without a clear idea of what we are taking them for.

Risk for risk's sake can even be a viable political strategy. When the inaction and infighting of traditional politicians frustrates us, candidates often emerge who promise "change" or that they will "shake things up." This refreshing message appeals to us because the status quo is not that great. Change can be a winning message even if we don't know what their policies are or what exactly will change. It is no wonder we often end up disappointed, because taking a risk on the unknown for its own sake is a bad risk strategy: it only creates uncertainty without the promise of a clearly defined reward.

It sounds simple, but knowing what you want might be the hardest part of risk management. People spend thousands of dollars on therapists and life coaches trying to figure out what they want out of life. While financial economics is no substitute for good therapy, it offers a method that can help define your goal, which, more than anything else, will increase your odds for a more successful outcome. This three-step process offers clarity and helps assess how much risk you might want to take to reach your goal.

1. What is your ultimate goal? If you achieve it, what does that look like?
2. How can you achieve your goal with no risk at all or as little risk as possible? In other words, what would guarantee you would accomplish your goal?
3. Is that no-risk option possible or desirable? If not, how much risk do you need to take to get what you want?

This process introduces you to a concept financial economists use every day: risk-free. The risk-free option is whatever delivers what you want with total certainty. If you are deciding what to do tonight and your objective is a pleasant evening, risk-free could be staying in and watching Netflix on the couch because you know how that will turn out. Risky is going out. Anything could happen: you might meet the love of your life or get hit by a car.

Risk-free looks different to each person, which is why figuring out what's risk-free for you provides clarity and helps you value risk. Simply articulating what you want and setting that as a goal is an extremely powerful tool. We often lionize risk takers, but the difference between who succeeds and who fails isn't who takes the boldest risks—it is who take smart risks, or risks with a clear objective. Take Kat Cole. She went from poverty to leading a billion-dollar company when she was barely thirty. She took what appeared to be one big risk after another to get there, but most of these paid off because Cole always knew exactly what she wanted and when a risk was worth taking.

THE MINIBON

Kat Cole might seem like someone born lucky. As the COO of Focus Brands, she runs well-known brands like Cinnabon and Auntie Anne's pretzels. Elegant and well-spoken, she divides her time between her homes in Atlanta and New York City when she's not traveling all over the world. Most people would never guess where Cole came from and what she had to overcome to achieve such success.

Cole made her name by shrinking Cinnabon's trademark product, its sugar-filled, buttery cinnamon roll. The original, beloved bun—all 880 calories of it—is the size of your face and absolutely delicious. Cole was thirty-two years old when she was hired in 2010. Cinnabon had had six years of net sales decline. The recession kept people out of malls and airports, and consumers claimed they wanted healthier choices. Cinnabon needed to shake things up: enter Project 599.

Project 599 aimed to reduce calories in the traditional Cinnabon with a product that clocked in under 600 calories. Research showed that offering lower-calorie alternatives could increase sales, but cutting calories required making a roll full of artificial sweeteners and stabilizers. Cole, who had been president of Cinnabon for barely a year at the time, killed the initiative. The new roll did not taste as good. She kept the original recipe instead and mandated that all franchise owners offer the 350-calorie MiniBon, a smaller version only the size of your fist. The petite rolls already existed, but fewer than 15 percent of Cinnabon stores sold them.

Franchise owners were skeptical. Cinnabon was famous for its large size. If the company sold a smaller version, it would have to offer it at a lower price—$2.50 instead of $3.60. If enough existing customers chose the mini instead of the original, it could mean smaller profits. The mini also required investing in new baking equipment. Cole believed that the smaller rolls would increase volume because they would attract new customers who didn't want a face-size cinnamon bun. She convinced franchise owners to take the risk and bet on volume. Her risk paid off: sales of the original barely dropped while overall sales rose 6 percent, due in large part to the mini. Cinnabon thrived, while similar fast-food companies floundered or failed.

Cole had a clear objective in mind: increase sales. Everyone at Cinnabon agreed on the problem: the high-calorie original roll didn't sell well in a more health-conscious market. Cole started by asking why Cinnabon was trying to reduce calories, and the executive team told her that "there was all this research that sales went up with a lower-calorie alternative." But "those were high-frequency snacks, like potato chips; no one eats a cinnamon roll every day," Cole explains. "That's not our model. We are in infrequent venues, like malls or airports. Our products are designed for the once-in-a-while, blow-your-socks-off indulgence. This was a problem because an artificially sweetened roll wouldn't be as yummy and it is still 599 calories."

Somehow the low-calorie option—not higher sales—had become the objective. Cole drove the point home by asking the people working on 599 "if they'd buy a 599-calorie roll that didn't taste good [and] everyone said no."

Cole says that when people need change they often "take a risk for risk's sake." This rarely goes well.

Doubling down on the decadence of a Cinnabon appeared to be a bold move for Cole, who was much younger than almost everyone she worked with. She was new to the company and new to fast food. Meanwhile, the rest of the fast-food industry was still trying to figure out low-calorie "healthful" menu options. At the time, choosing to stick with a calorie-dense/high-calorie product seemed like a major risk, one Cole bet her career on.

You can see the concept of risk-free at work in Cole's decision process. First, she identified the goal—increase sales in a changing market. Notice how she avoided the option that stymied her competitors—create a healthy alternative. Doing nothing might appear to be risk-free, but it would not achieve her goal because sales would continue to decline.

Then Cole hit upon the lowest-risk option that would increase sales. Her colleagues had thought a diet pastry was the answer because everyone else in the industry was offering low-calorie versions of their products. But Cole saw that path as a bigger risk because a new product was not guaranteed to increase sales and risked diminishing the brand, which was all about quality and decadence.

So if a new product wasn't the solution, then "the only way to reduce calories was to be smaller or have different ingredients," she explains. The smaller roll was already on the market; some franchises had been selling it for almost a decade. Working with an existing product rather than changing the recipe of a beloved product was actually less risky than it seemed, especially because there was evidence from some franchises that the smaller roll would sell, and it did not compromise the company's reputation. Based on the data, adding the smaller cinnamon roll was the least risky way to go if the goal was to increase sales, and it worked. Within a few years, revenues doubled and Cinnabon became a billion-dollar brand.

Cole learned about managing risk by making unconventional choices early in life. She had a chaotic childhood with an alcoholic father. Her dad earned a decent living, thanks to a good white-collar job, which was unusual since both sides of the extended family lived in trailers and shacks. With no way to support herself outside of the relationship, Cole's mother made the tough decision to leave, taking her daughters with her. She worked multiple jobs, while keeping the family on a tight $10-a-week food budget for four people and relying on young Kat, the eldest, only nine at the time. Armed with a list of tasks, Kat ran the household, and in the process learned that taking risks often means you need to "work your butt off" to make it happen. "I could not have known the valuable business lesson it was at that time. The belief it was possible to make unpopular and nontraditional choices and have it work out."

Cole chose a stable career path, majoring in engineering at the University of North Florida, with aspirations to be a corporate lawyer. To support her studies, she worked as a waitress at Hooters, the restaurant chain famous for uniformed waitresses in tight shirts and orange micro shorts.

Cole was a great waitress. When the bartender couldn't work because her son was sick, Cole tended bar. When the kitchen staff walked out because the chefs wouldn't work overtime, Cole fried the wings. When Hooters corporate asked the manager who was the franchise's best employee, the manager named Cole. Hooters needed someone to go to Australia and train employees at a new franchise, so they asked Cole. "I said yes, to go to Australia. I didn't have a passport; I'd never been on a plane; I'd never been out of the country. But I still said yes and then I worked my ass off."

Cole thrived in the role and soon Hooters was flying her all over the world to help set up new franchises. But her schoolwork suffered and she started failing classes. She had to make a choice: drop out of college and give up on her dream of becoming a corporate lawyer or stop traveling for Hooters.

Both Bill Gates and Mark Zuckerberg dropped out of college, and they became billionaires, but Cole wasn't dropping out of Harvard with powerful and connected friends, nor did she have an affluent family to fall back on. She wasn't going to Silicon Valley, where dropping out of college is considered by some to be a badge of honor. In her world, college was the surest path to success and stability, and she would be giving it up to be paid hourly at Hooters. It may sound like a risky decision, but Cole's goal was to get a good job one day and achieve the security and stability she lacked as a child. At first, she thought that meant practicing corporate law, but then she realized that being a lawyer was not the ultimate goal—it was just one way to get there. And someone was offering her a path to what she ultimately wanted, even if it was not the way most people got it. She dropped out. Not everyone would have seen this so clearly; to many of us it would seem like a risky choice.

Cole was able to see that dropping out was the right decision because it felt right, and it turned out to be low-risk for her objective. "It was not that difficult a decision and not one that felt that risky because I had a compelling alternative," she remembers. "I wasn't sitting around thinking . . . mmm . . . I am not sure college is for me. . . . I'll do something else. I was traveling around the world and was good at it. . . . I was doing something I loved, I had an opportunity to keep doing it, but there were no guarantees. I had no contract. I was an hourly employee. No one sat me down and said this is your career path; you can bank on this. But it was so right."

Cole worked so many hours she managed to pull in $45,000 a year. Eventually, Hooters corporate headquarters offered her a salaried job for $22,000 that she accepted because it was her chance to climb the corporate ladder to an executive position. Cole rose through the ranks and was an executive vice president by the time she was twenty-six. She may have been a college dropout, but the sort of companies that usually hire only Ivy League graduates were now trying to recruit her for high-flying jobs in private equity and management. She stuck with Hooters, "even though it was sort of embarrassing every time I handed someone my business card."

Even though she did not have an undergraduate degree, Cole eventually earned an MBA. By 2010, she was a star in the restaurant industry, and she got an offer that was too good to turn down, the chance to run Cinnabon.

Cole's early choices might have seemed risky at the time to outsiders, but she owes her success to taking risks in a smart way. Her success comes down to being good at identifying her goal and the least risky way to get it. She didn't think twice about dropping out of college or yanking Project 599. For most of us, the path is not always so clear.

Knowing what you want is hard, especially when you know change is what you need. In financial economics, the first step is to identify your goal and price it in risk-free terms. There is an investment known as the risk-free asset that offers investors something no other asset can: predictability. In finance, risk-free promises a certain payoff no matter what happens. If markets crash, you know what you'll get paid. If markets boom, you only get paid what you were initially promised. The price of that risk-free asset is the most critical piece of information in any investment problem, or any decision, you might face.

THE PRICE OF RISK-FREE

Suppose your family's vacation next summer will cost $3,000. If you need $3,000 in the near future, you should invest your vacation money in a safe place; you won't want to lose a dime in the market. It could be a simple savings account or a Treasury bill. Each offers a set interest rate for a certain amount of time. To have about $3,000 when summer rolls around, you would need to invest $2,970 at 1 percent interest for one year.

Risky, in this case, is everything else—long-term bonds, stocks, gold, Bitcoin—all of which offer a much higher expected return and a chance your $2,970 will be $6,000 in six months. But there is also a chance markets will crash and you'll only have $500 for the family vacation.

If your goal is $3,000 for a vacation next year, your risk-free option is the savings account that pays 1 percent interest. Figuring this out before you invest serves two important functions.

First, it helps you gauge how much risk you need to take to achieve your goal. Suppose someone offers you an investment that is guaranteed to double your money in one year (actually, you should run far away and warn all your friends and family to avoid this person—but for the sake of argument let's assume this offer is legitimate). If this investment really exists, there is no need to risk losing your money in the stock market, and you only need to save $1,500 for your family vacation. The risk-free rate puts a cost on getting what you want for certain. If you only have $1,500, you can't afford risk-free, so you can either take more risk or take a less expensive vacation.

Second, and more important, the process of defining risk-free helps to clarify your objectives. Defining what risk-free means to you forces you to think through what you want and what will happen when you get it. The 1 percent return is how much money you will have in one year. If you have $2,000 today, it will be $2,020 next year; if you have $2,970, you know you'll have enough for your vacation.

But it can be hard to see the risk-free choice because there is no single universal risk-free asset; it depends on your goal. For most of us, dropping out of college would be risky. But for Cole, dropping out of college was a lower-risk choice than years of school and debt to be a corporate lawyer, because she had a specific goal in mind—an executive job— and someone was offering her a way to get it when she was nineteen.

Articulating your goal and putting a risk-free price on it are the first steps of good risk taking.

Risk-free is different for everyone because it depends on your goal. That's true even in finance.

RISK-FREE FOR ME, BUT NOT FOR THEE

Suppose you want to take your partner on the trip of a lifetime when you retire in twenty years. You estimate it will cost $30,000.

Having $30,000 in twenty years, risk-free, is more complicated. You need to make sure you don't lose the money in markets and that your savings keep up with inflation. If inflation averages 2 percent a year* for twenty years, $30,000 today will only be worth about $20,000 when you take that trip. The bank account you use to save for the family vacation isn't risk-free for a twenty-year investment because the interest rate it pays probably won't keep up with inflation. The risk-free financial asset for the retirement vacation is a twenty-year bond that ensures your investment return keeps up with inflation.

Defining our goal in risk-free terms can help us gain clarity in any life decision. We all have friends who desperately want to get married and figure that the risk-free way to achieve this is to marry the first person who loves them dearly, even if they don't return the feeling. In fact, they feel safer because they assume this person will never leave them, so they'll never get hurt. But often their marriage lacks a strong mutual connection and is not hardy enough to weather life's challenges, and they divorce. If simply *getting married* is their goal, then it is a risk-free choice to wed the first person who loves them. But if their goal is *being married,* then settling is a high-risk choice.

---

* The inflation rate is risky too; it could be more or less than 2 percent.

Consider another life decision: Suppose you find your dream house in a hot real estate market. If your goal is getting that specific house, the risk-free option is putting in a large bid, maybe above the asking price, as much as you are prepared to pay (assuming you aren't paying more than you can afford)—to ensure you get it. This will eliminate the risk of being outbid, even if you overpay. If this is the only house you love and plan to live in for the rest of your life, overpaying is the price you pay for the certainty of not losing a bidding war.

But if you want to get a good bargain to make money on this investment, or if you plan to sell the house in the foreseeable future, then your goal is different, and so is your risk-free strategy. If the goal is paying as little as possible instead of getting that one perfect house, then you should bid less than what you think the house is worth and be comfortable with the risk of losing a bidding war. Otherwise you risk overpaying and losing money when you sell the house.

People often confuse the two goals and underbid on a house they really want or else get caught up in the market frenzy and pay too much for a house they plan to sell in five years.

Suppose you are thinking about taking a new job. You are comfortable in your current job; you have an understanding boss who lets you leave early when you need to be home; and you've mastered the skills your position requires. If your goal is advancing your career or earning a bigger salary, then staying in your present job won't get you what you want and may even be riskier than making a switch. Changing jobs forces you to broaden your network and learn new skills, all of which can enhance your career, boost your earnings, and make you more employable in the future. But if your goal is work-life balance, leaving is a big risk since your new boss may not tolerate the other demands in your life. Mastering the new skills and company politics requires putting in more hours. The risky choice depends on your goal.

Often we must balance competing objectives—a house we love and got for a good price, a stable career that offers both work-life balance and an opportunity for advancement. But first thinking through what you are looking for and putting it in risk-free terms helps you to refine your goal and acknowledge how much risk you are willing to take.

Anyone can take a risk. But doing so with a clear goal takes conviction and focus. It requires knowing exactly what you want, and few of us do. One of Cole's favorite catchphrases is to focus on things that are "small enough to change but big enough to matter." In other words, take the lowest-risk path to achieve your goal.

Figuring out what we want and putting it in risk-free terms should be the first step in assessing any risk problem. But sometimes, perhaps most of the time, we identify the low-risk choice and it isn't what we want or we can't afford it. Take the dream-house example: If you can't afford overpaying, you have to take the risk of losing the bidding war. The following chapter explores the next step, figuring out when to take more risk.

Chapter 3

TAKING A RISK:
When to Reject Safety and Go for More

The dangers of life are infinite,
and among them is safety.

—GOETHE

Learning how to define your goal and price it in risk-free terms is the foundation of any good risk strategy. But what happens when we don't want to choose the risk-free option? Maybe it is too expensive, or we crave more risk and the possibility of more reward. We tend to think of taking a risk as a binary choice: either we take a risk or we don't. But smart risk taking involves going for more, and taking just enough risk that we need to, or are comfortable with, to achieve our goal. Calibrating the right amount of risk is the next step, but if we haven't defined our goal and priced it in risk-free terms first, we set ourselves up for failure.

I made this mistake in a pretty painful way. Most retirement economists are cautious, risk-averse government workers or professors: they don't conduct their research in brothels. I did not plan to end up on this path. I got here because I took a big risk early in my career without a clear goal or understanding of what risk-free meant to me.

SOMETIMES EVEN ECONOMISTS GET RISK-FREE WRONG

At the start of 2006, I was rushing through Copley Place in Boston wearing a stiff suit and snow boots, carrying high heels in a plastic bag. I saw a sign with an arrow below: "Barneys [the high-end department store] interviews this way."

On a whim, I followed the arrow to a room where a well-dressed woman was sitting at a desk. "So, I am here interviewing to be an economics professor," I said, then lowered my voice. "But just between us, I don't think it's for me. Can I have an interview to work at Barneys?"

She looked at me blankly before another well-dressed woman, who was waiting for her interview, said in an indignant tone, "You can't just come in off the street and interview. I sent my résumé in weeks ago."

Dejected, I left and went to my scheduled interview. I didn't get that job either.

Persuing an economics PhD was one of the biggest risks I ever took, and it was my first that seemed to blow up. A few months after that day in Boston, after six long years of hard work, I was set to graduate without a job or any plan for the future.

There are worse things in life than being a young, healthy Ivy League graduate without a job in hand. But in my field, having a degree but no job is a big deal, and after years in graduate school, I'd lost all perspective. I had come to rely on economics to explain everything, believing the economy and my life were under control. I loved the order economic models imposed on a chaotic world. Many models assume that if you do X, Y will happen: if you tax less, the economy will grow; if you cut interest rates, unemployment will fall. It became a religion for me. If I worked hard, I'd get a job. When I didn't, I was devastated.

I had been drawn to economics in the first place after growing up in a community with lots of poverty. Economics offered the answers about job loss and inequality that I was searching for, so I started graduate school with lots of passion for the subject. But I was totally unprepared for a mathematics-based PhD. Most people wouldn't dream of taking on a quantitative PhD without at least majoring in math in college, but I went for it anyway.

I struggled the first year, barely sleeping to work my way through entire math textbooks just to finish my assignments; I nearly failed out. The challenge inspired me to double down: I was determined to not only finish my degree but also be the best at it. I chose the safest, most employable research topic I could think of—the economics of retirement.

Most twenty-three-year-olds would probably choose a sexier topic, but I was captivated by the concept of retirement. To me it was the purest and most beautiful of all economic problems: What is the best way to move resources into the future? How do you decide how much to save now versus later?

This is the simplest and yet most complex question economists, or anyone, must answer. I distilled it into one elegant math problem that described exactly how much people should save in a controlled risk environment. Most economics dissertations don't include a math problem this hard, but I was still reeling from being the weakest math student. If I worked hard and solved this very difficult problem, then I'd be assured of success—at least that's what I thought. Solving a hard math problem became my risk strategy, even though I was not quite sure what success meant to me.

I shut myself away in the library and spent the better part of my twenties isolated, trying to solve that single math problem. Five years later, when I actually solved it, I expected something wonderful to happen; instead, everything fell apart. My relationship with my adviser deteriorated, and the sudden death of a close friend left me emotionally shattered. My worst enemy, however, was my ambivalence.

Most PhD candidates aspire for a job in academia. This is the standard goal by which you measure success. As crazy as it sounds, after all those years, I had never questioned that goal until I found myself in interviews to be an economics professor and kept hearing a voice inside my head shouting *"Run!"*

So, no surprise, I torpedoed all of my interviews and, with them, my default life plan. It was drummed into me in graduate school that the risk-free choice was to take a tenure-track position. Nothing else was worth doing, and if you left academia you could *never* come back. So walking away from the only world I knew as an adult—not to mention job security—was a cosmic step.

As a frustrated STEM (science, technology, engineering, mathematics) graduate in the midst of an economic boom, I made a counterintuitive decision to enter journalism, even though the industry was floundering at the time and my writing style was—to put it kindly—academic. This time, though, I had a clear objective: avoid math, have fun, and spend time with people. For these goals, journalism was the risk-free option. Many publications were just launching their online editions in 2006, so they weren't too particular about who wrote for their websites. The *Economist* gave me an unpaid shot and I took it. I had no idea where it would lead, or how long I could afford to work for no money (an odd choice for a pension expert who always thinks about financing the future), but I took a chance and hoped it would work out.

In the meantime, a friend showed my dissertation with the complicated retirement math problem to Robert C. Merton, a Nobel Prize–winning financial economist. Shortly after that, he offered me a job. Together we developed strategies to help people invest for retirement. He became the mentor I'd never had and taught me finance.

Working with him completely changed how I thought about economics and how I made life decisions. I was able to identify the mistakes I had made in calculating risk.

By jumping into a hard, time-consuming degree without any idea what I wanted from it, I had taken a risk without a clear goal. I never figured out what risk-free meant to me. I had assumed it was more education—the harder, the better—but that's not always true, especially for advanced, specialized degrees. The risk-free asset I had invested in was an academic job.

I didn't gauge how much risk I wanted to take. I expected more from my career and was willing to take risks to get it. I did not want the risk-free option—something I didn't realize until I tried to interview at Barneys. But, full of doubt, I was not confident about the decision, which prevented me from moving forward.

I don't regret going to graduate school because it offered me some amazing opportunities, including, eventually, the career I wanted. But had I known I was chasing the wrong risk-free goal from the start, I would have managed my risks better and been prepared for the possibility that my career might take an unconventional path. I still would have gone to graduate school but with a nonacademic job in mind from the start. Taking a different approach, I would have done internships outside of government or academia; that way, I would have known how much risk I could manage as I sampled offerings in fields outside of my comfort zone. I struggled to get my first job because I lacked clarity and confidence. All I knew was either you followed the prescribed safe path or you stepped into some dark unknown. If I had been honest with myself from the beginning that academia was not for me, I would have done a better job calibrating my risks and saved myself—and many interviewers—lots of time.

When we chase the wrong goal and take a risk, odds are it won't go well. In what life challenge do people get risk-free wrong more than in any other? My first love, the retirement problem. By the time I started working with Merton, I had been researching retirement for years and thought I understood it pretty well. But he reframed the retirement problem for me in terms I'd never considered before, by spelling out what risk-free means in retirement and from there how to manage risk. This strategy changed how I saw everything.

RISK-FREE RETIREMENT

When you sit down with a financial planner and she asks you, "What is your risk tolerance?," she typically means how much money can you tolerate losing. But this is the wrong question. It does not address your saving goal: being able to retire one day. A better question to get at your goal in risk-free terms is "How much income will you need in retirement, and how much income do you want?"

The financial industry was set up in large part to maintain and grow wealth for things like trust funds and large endowments. When our system of employer-provided pensions changed to employee-managed retirement savings accounts, the financial industry simply took this trust-fund investment strategy and offered it to the average person, but giving everyone the same strategy led households astray.

Remember, in order to figure out what risk-free is, we need to start with a goal. Average people and trust funders are not solving the same problem. Trust funders want to build a fortune that lasts for generations. For the rest of us, the goal is to save when we are young and spend when we are old. This problem requires a totally different solution than growing and maintaining wealth over generations—and to make matters worse, it is a much harder problem to solve. You don't know how long your money needs to last, and if you spend too much you risk poverty in your most vulnerable years.

Conventional wisdom in the financial industry is to build up as much wealth as possible (the trust-fund strategy) and then to spend a certain percent, say 4 percent, each year once you retire. But the 4 percent per year isn't a fixed amount—the actual amount you receive depends on what's happening in the stock market. That's where the strategy goes wrong. A predictable salary, like the one you earned when you were working, should be the goal of your retirement fund. Most workers wouldn't accept a salary that varies with stock prices—why should retirees?

You are exposed to more risk than you realize in retirement because the financial industry has defined risk-free wrong. You might think risk-free retirement means investing in short-term government bonds or cash because, just like the summer vacation savings account we discussed in chapter 2, these investments don't lose money. And there is a good chance your retirement account is invested with a strategy called a target date fund. It mitigates the risk your portfolio will lose money as you age by taking your money out of stocks and investing it in short-term bonds; because short-term bond prices are fairly stable and predictable, your balance won't fluctuate too much. This strategy offers some certainty about how much money you will have saved on the day you retire.

But it does not offer any certainty about how much you can actually spend each year, because you can't predict how long you will live or what the market will do to your savings during retirement. We can buy that certainty from an insurance company by purchasing a fixed, or simple life, annuity: you hand over your savings to an insurance company and it pays you a fixed amount* every year for as long as you and/or your partner live after you retire. This is as close to risk-free as retirement gets, delivering the goal of predictable income for every year you live, versus a lump amount saved up to day one of retirement that you still have to manage.

An important caveat to the risk-free option of owning an annuity is that buying one is not necessarily risk-free. Annuity prices are based on long-term interest rates. The lower the interest rates, the less income you get from an insurance company. Suppose you spend your

---

* Can be indexed to inflation.

working years with a single goal: $1 million in the bank on the day you retire. In 2000, when ten-year real interest rates were 4.4 percent, $1 million would buy you a twenty-year inflation-adjusted annuity that paid out $75,000 a year. In 2017, when real ten-year interest rates were 0.43 percent, that $1 million would buy you only $52,000 a year. It is impossible to know what is the best day to buy an annuity, and it can mean the difference between eating sea bass at a nice restaurant or canned tuna throughout your golden years. But what you can do is invest in long-term bonds as your risk-free asset. Investing for income in a low-risk way requires changing your portfolio strategy from short-term to long-term bonds so your wealth moves with annuity prices. Conventional wisdom tells you that short-term bonds are low risk because they ensure your asset balance won't change very much, but they actually can be risky when your goal is retirement income because they don't keep up with annuity prices.*

An annuity premium is the price of risk-free retirement. Now you need to figure out two things: Do you want the risk-free strategy? If you want it, can you afford the price? Unfortunately, most of us cannot afford to save enough for a risk-free retirement. Annuities are expensive and bonds that hedge annuity prices don't pay much interest. Most people need to take more risk and invest in stocks too.

While buying an annuity is not right for everyone, annuity prices offer an invaluable data point. In the United States, many 401(k) statements now display your balance in income terms, using an annuity price. It is the price of a risk-free retirement. This price tells you how much you can spend without risk. For example, knowing you'll have $52,000 a year to live off each year is more meaningful than $1 million in the bank. The amount of risk-free income your wealth can buy is the foundation of any spending plan, whether or not you buy an annuity. If, for instance, you only have enough saved to buy an annuity that pays

---

* If you don't buy an annuity, you can invest in long-term bonds and achieve a similar level of income predictability.

$52,000 a year and you want to spend $70,000, you know you need to take some risk to have the income you desire.

The annuity price helps you gauge how much risk you can bear or need to take in the market. Suppose of that $70,000, you estimate you need $50,000 a year for necessities, such as your car or your home, and $20,000 for more discretionary expenses, such as travel and eating out. It makes sense to invest about 30 percent of your retirement money in something risky, to finance the $20,000 in discretionary expenses and invest the rest in risk-free assets, such as long-term bonds or an annuity. This strategy ensures you can meet all your necessary expenses no matter what happens to the market and still offers some reward on what you can risk.

The conversation you need to have with your financial planner concerning retirement is not how you feel about risk; instead, you should talk about how much income you can gamble. This type of discussion not only helps you plan for retirement but also changes the way you invest and approach risk.

Chapter 4

RISK MEASUREMENT:
Hollywood's Never-Ending Quest for Certainty

Il n'est pas certain que tout soit incertain.
(It is not certain that everything is uncertain.)

—BLAISE PASCAL, *PENSÉES*

Risk-free is a single, predictable outcome. Risk is the opposite, all the things that might happen and the odds that they will. In a perfect world, we have a risk estimate that captures all possible outcomes and puts precise odds on each one happening. But the world is full of uncertainty, and we lack the imagination to anticipate everything that could go wrong (or right) and rarely know the exact odds of anything. All we can do is take a guess, and often the most scientific way to do so is to make a risk estimate: data from the past is analyzed and a range of things that might happen in the future is produced, along with estimates of the probability of their occurrence.

Sometimes it is easy to make an accurate estimate; at other times risk measurement is nearly impossible. When it comes to the challenges of measuring risk, I can think of no better example than the movie business. One of the hardest risk measurement problems that has eluded generations of risk modelers is putting a number on the odds that a movie will be a hit.

THE LAND OF BROKEN RISK MODELS

Hollywood is often called the land of broken dreams, and anywhere bets go so wrong so often is fertile ground for our risk exploration. Every day young, hopeful, talented people come to Hollywood hoping to make it big. But few realize these dreams and leave with bitterness and regret instead. Hollywood could also be called the land of broken risk models. Investors, including banks, hedge funds, and insurance companies, have a long history of coming to Hollywood thinking they can tame the market with science and data, which also often ends in tears or lawsuits. There is a saying in Hollywood financial circles: "The secret to making lots of money is come here with three times that amount."

A recent casualty is Ryan Kavanaugh, a Los Angeles native who charmed Hollywood with talk of his Monte Carlo simulation* that lived in an elaborate Excel spreadsheet and promised to make the unpredictable predictable. He claimed his model could forecast which movies would do well and which ones would bomb. It was a seductive pitch.

Such predictability is seductive because it is so elusive in Hollywood. If past performance is any predictor of success, investors would have stayed far away, but everyone in Hollywood is looking for the next big thing in a sea of random outcomes. Like others before it, Kavanaugh's model eventually failed, but not before many investors bought in.

People in the movie business explain that it is impossible to predict what will be a blockbuster or a flop. Each film is like a small business

---

* A numeric simulation technique commonly used in the finance industry. It simulates a range of potential future outcomes.

with hundreds of moving parts. The only way to manage risk is to make lots of movies; most won't make money, but a few will hit it big and pay for the others. This is a risky way to run a business, and it also explains why there are so many bad movies, with terrible, derivative plots, that fail at the box office. Every year brings both a notorious clunker that cost hundreds of millions to make and an independent drama, with a great script, that cost only $10 million and earned $300 million.

This bet-on-'em-all strategy is a colossal waste of money and talent. Many great movies are never made while billions are squandered on bombs that people forget as soon as they leave the theater.

Predicting winners is an especially hard risk problem. In most businesses, decision makers can rely on data from the past to help them figure out the more fruitful investments that will pay off in the future. A good risk estimate requires data that can do two things: (1) reveal lessons from the past that will be relevant in the future, and (2) predict that certain past outcomes are more likely than others. The nature of moviemaking means its business data lacks both of those things.

To make matters worse, filmmaking is a particularly risky venture requiring a large up-front investment that doesn't pay off for years, if it ever does. Studios scramble to reduce financial risk by securing financing from outsiders to take on the risk for them. Attracting these investors often involves piggybacking off the latest fad, signing a megastar to the project, or seeking the potential for merchandising revenue. These strategies are assumed to increase the odds of making money, but they don't necessarily increase the odds that a movie will be good or even profitable.*

Investors who finance the films usually get equity, meaning they get a share of the film's profits after writers, actors, directors, production

---

* According to Nick Meaney, CEO of Epagogix, a consultancy that uses machine learning to improve scripts, hiring a star does not increase the odds of profitability, and the star's high price tag rarely pays off.

crew, and editors are paid.* Because the expected return on most movies is less than zero, the investors shoulder most of the financial risk for next to no reward. To offset the risk, deals are often made for a slate of about a dozen movies at a time, but investors often cannot choose which films are included in the slate.

It seems baffling that anyone would agree to these terms, but investing in movies is exciting and sexy; you get to hang out with movie stars and go to film premieres. Matthew Lieberman, an executive at PricewaterhouseCoopers, says clients looking to get into movies are often sophisticated investors who become blinded by the glamour of Hollywood—attending award shows, hobnobbing with celebrities—and make investments they would never consider in other markets.

If someone could come up with a way to scientifically pick winners, then a well-functioning moviemaking market would be ripe for the taking. Enter Ryan Kavanaugh.

He grew up in Los Angeles as part of a privileged family and started a venture capital fund with his father after college that raised money from the biggest players in Hollywood to invest in start-ups during the 1990s. The firm fell apart after the dot-com bust in 2000, and Kavanaugh was sued by his investors.

Just a few years later he made a comeback and cofounded Relativity Media in 2004 before he turned thirty. Armed with a team of number crunchers, he marketed himself as a math whiz in jeans who could provide the predictability Hollywood and his investors craved. His timing couldn't have been better because movie studios needed a new source of financing in the mid-2000s. For years they had depended on a German tax shelter to attract investors and off-load some of the considerable financial risk involved with making movies. But Angela Merkel's coalition government nixed the shelter after she took office in 2005.

The German tax shelter had given investors and studios some

---

* Sometimes small independent film producers offer scope for risk reduction: studios can off-load their financial risk onto them.

financial incentive to invest in films, so losing it left studios unsure how to get financing. In the meantime, hedge funds were looking to invest in high-yield risky assets. It was a perfect match. Kavanaugh jumped on the opportunity, especially since hedge funds, with their roots in finance, have to put a number on any risk they take. He offered investors the two things they wanted. He gave them the glamour they craved. An entertainment lawyer who has worked with Kavanaugh told the *New Yorker* in 2012, "Ryan knows how to suck people into the glamour of Hollywood. You're a banker, leading a dull life, and all of a sudden you're hanging out with movie stars. You think, I'm walking down the beach with Gerard Butler! Before you know it, you're rationalizing why you should be making this investment."

And most critically, Kavanaugh claimed he could put a reliable number on risk, precisely what the institutional investors needed to hear before they put their clients' money on the line to make movies. Kavanaugh would go to New York, visit the banks and hedge funds, talk the finance talk, and write equations on a whiteboard to put precise odds on whether or not a movie would make money.

The hedge fund managers needed this because measuring risk is what people in finance do. They feel more comfortable when they can put odds on success. We all do.

TURNING DATA INTO RISK: WHAT NORMALLY HAPPENS

No matter what type of decision you need to make—momentous or mundane—the simplest way to measure risk is to consider what happened in the past and assume something similar will happen in the future. This gives us a reliable estimate of the range of things that might occur.

If you drive to the same airport once a month, odds are it does not take exactly thirty-three minutes each time. More likely, it usually takes between twenty and forty minutes, depending on traffic or weather. That range doesn't account for something unusual happening, like a terrible accident that causes an hour's delay. In general, we make a decision based on the normal range of things that might happen. If we are prudent, we assume it will take forty minutes to get to the airport; if we can tolerate a little risk, we might only allow for thirty minutes.

Risk is our guess about what the future holds; more precisely, it is the *range* of things that might happen and how probable each event is. The odds of guessing a single outcome correctly—for example, that a movie will earn $200 million—is nearly impossible (even Kavanaugh did not promise he could do it), but the odds are we can figure out a range of possible outcomes that could happen. A summer blockbuster has an excellent chance of earning between $1 million and $4 billion at the American box office. Four billion dollars is possible, but it's a long shot, and a summer release will almost certainly earn more than $1 million, so making a good risk assessment requires narrowing the range of possibilities.

You need a workable range for any risky decision. If you anticipated a three-hundred-car pileup whenever you drove to the airport, you'd always leave three hours in advance and in almost every instance end up wasting your valuable time sitting around an empty terminal.

The hard part is knowing what constitutes a reasonable range. Is twenty to forty minutes enough, or is traffic so unpredictable that you need fifty minutes or even three hours?

In financial economics, determining the ideal range is done a little more methodically. Estimating the range of what might happen using data is called risk measurement. Risk measurement, as we know it, is a recent human invention. Until the end of the Renaissance and the start of the Enlightenment, most people presumed uncertainty was determined by divine forces and couldn't be measured. But in the seventeenth century the mathematicians Blaise Pascal and Pierre de

Fermat started measuring probabilities for games involving dice. Their insight changed how scholars thought of risk: they started to view it as something that could be measured and controlled.

The mathematician Jakob Bernoulli took their contributions further about sixty years later, applying these burgeoning lessons to the real world, outside of the controlled situations with precise, quantifiable odds used thus far. He assumed the range of things that happened in the past could be used to predict the odds that something will happen in the future. One of his major contributions was the law of large numbers, which says if you repeat an experiment enough times, you can estimate accurate probabilities of what might happen in the future.

These pioneering statisticians provided the bedrock of modern statistics, the study of how we measure risk based on what happened in the past. For example, consider a stock price and how much it went up on down from one month to the next. The figure below shows how much stock prices, the S&P 500, went up or down each month between 1950 and 2018. Think of it as 824 trips to the airport, only for monthly stock

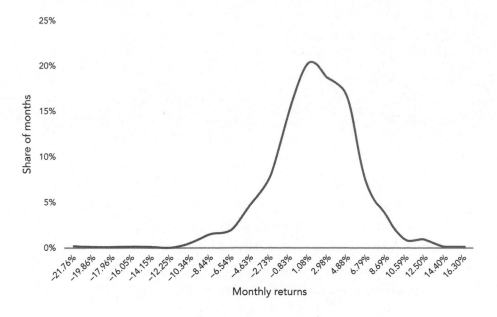

returns. If you assume the future will be like the past, the figure on the previous page shows everything that could happen to the stock market in the next sixty-nine years and the odds that it will happen.

Notice the shape of this figure and how most stock returns cluster in toward the middle. In most months the stock market returns between –11 percent and 13 percent; a 16 percent return is very rare.

Financial economics often assumes the history of stock returns conforms to a certain shape called a normal distribution or bell curve. It is smooth and symmetrical, and most of the data is clustered in the middle. It looks like the figure below.

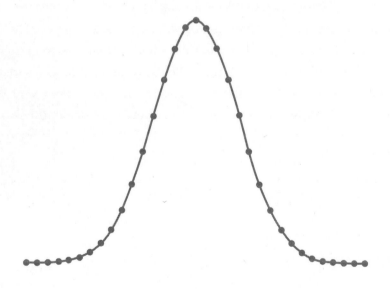

If you believe that the range of what can happen looks normal, you can make a quick estimate of risk. This is called a standard deviation, or volatility. Volatility tells you the range in which stock returns will vary most of the time. Or to be exact, in any given month, 68 percent of the time, the U.S. stock market will fall 3 percent or rise 5 percent, or some percentage in between. The bigger the range is, the riskier the stock portfolio (or any type of risk) is, because you can expect a wider possibility of things to typically happen. Investing in emerging-market stocks is riskier than investing in American stocks: prices will probably fall 8 percent or go up 9 percent, or some percentage in between.

If you were superneurotic about getting to the airport, you could use the same technique. Suppose you drove to the airport nine hundred times and estimate airport-travel volatility: the range of time it usually takes to get there is twenty to forty minutes. You'd also notice that a three-hour airport trip caused by a major traffic accident is less probable. It only happens 1–2 percent of the time. The traffic accident is called a "tail risk" because a three-hour trip is so unlikely it is in the tail of normal distribution.

These measurements are how people in finance define risk: they often assume a normal distribution and use volatility as the standard measure of risk. You can probably find a volatility estimate on your mutual fund statement. It tells you, roughly, how much you can expect the mutual fund to go up and down in price. It assumes a close to normal distribution. But it does not tell you much about tail risk, which, though improbable, could be a catastrophic outcome, like the stock market falling 40 percent.

Normality is a controversial assumption, and lots of evidence points to stock returns not conforming to this shape. If returns aren't normal, then the range associated with volatility will understate the risk. So in our airport-travel example, a trip may take twenty to forty minutes only 50 percent of the time. Or the tail risk, the nightmare three-hour trip, may be more likely than you expect, with a three-hundred-car pileup happening 5 percent of the time.

Making movies in Hollywood is just like traffic: there is nothing normal about it.

THE MOVIE BUSINESS: SKEW YOU

Typically, it is hard to measure risk in the movie business because it is nearly impossible to pin down a reasonable range. A movie is like an airport trip that will take anywhere between ten minutes and two hours.

If you plot the history of movie profits, it looks totally different from the normal distribution shape assumed in finance.

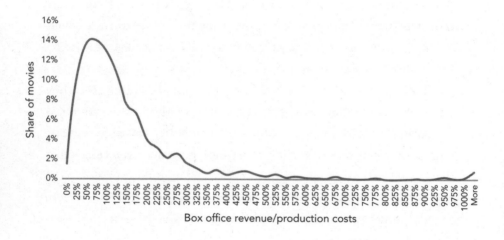

The figure above shows the ratio of box office revenues (foreign and domestic) to production costs for all movies released and shown in at least one hundred U.S. theaters between 2008 and 2017. Any value less than 100 percent means ticket sales did not cover the costs of production. To cover marketing and additional costs not related to production, a good rule of thumb is that a movie must make double its production costs to be profitable.*

For decades, box office returns have had the same risk profile,

---

* This does not include marketing costs and revenue from DVD sales, streaming, and TV; this figure measures only how much of the production costs are recouped at the box office.

despite the introductions of innovations like IMAX and competition from streaming and better-quality TVs. The economists Arthur De Vany and W. David Walls looked at box office receipts of 2,015 movies between 1985 and 1996 and plotted almost the exact same shape.

The figure is known as a skewed distribution. It is what makes the movie business the movie business. It also describes many decisions we face every day.

The asymmetric shape shows how risky and unpredictable the movie business is. If there's a normal distribution and the center falls on break-ing even, there are an equal number of profit-making and money-losing scenarios, and most movies fall within a close range of breaking even. With a positive-skewed distribution, like the previous one illustrating the movie business, the range of possibilities is large; there are far more profitable scenarios than money-losing ones. Notice the long tail on the right, which covers the range of potential positive profits. A movie in this range could barely break even or return more than 1000 percent, or anything in between. All the profitable scenarios are equally unlikely. The odds are a movie will lose money because most are clustered in the smaller, loss part of the curve. Fifty-three percent of movies shown don't earn back production budgets at the box office, and that's assum-ing they are shown in many theaters (most movies aren't). And even if they do make a profit at the box office, their earning potential looks like a complete crapshoot with only a few big winners.

"Skewness" poses problems for measuring risk. For volatility to tell what will happen most of the time, you need a normal, symmetric distri-bution. If your distribution is skewed, volatility underestimates risk; it might only tell you what will happen 30–40 percent of the time. The long tail contains a huge range of possibilities; all are nearly equally probable and unlikely. Studios know that most movies will lose money, but that a few will be at the end of long tail and subsidize all the losers, but they don't know which ones those will be or have any idea if they will be a mild or huge success.

It's common for risk to be skewed; the symmetric distribution is called normal, but it is not always common. Aspiring movie stars who come to Hollywood face a positive-skewed distribution. Odds are they will never make it, but there is a large range of potential working-actor scenarios that have a small chance of happening, from landing regular bit parts in movies to becoming the next megastar.

Suppose you are thinking of leaving your steady, well-paying job to work at a new tech start-up. It pays less than your current position, but you get valuable stock options. Think through the range of bad things that could happen: the start-up might go bust or you might make less money for a few years and eventually leave. On the flip side, many good things could happen: the start-up could be the next Google and you'll get rich; or maybe the company will be bought out and a nice windfall comes your way, but you still have to find another job; or maybe the start-up will grow into a bigger company and one day pay you what you earn now, but you'll have more responsibility. While it looks like there are more good outcomes than bad ones, the bad outcomes are more probable because most start-ups will fail. If you plotted the range of things that could happen, it would look like a skewed distribution instead of a normal distribution. A bulk of the distribution is in the loss zone, but there is a long tail extending into all the successful but unlikely scenarios.

Actually, the investment strategies of venture capital firms, which put their money in start-ups, are similar to those of movie studios. Many of their investments lose money, but the odd unicorn pays off to make up for the losers. Kavanaugh's history in venture capital was good preparation for convincing people to invest in long shots. The skewed distribution in this industry also explains why millions of dollars are poured into dud tech firms that are clearly a bad idea.

Kavanaugh claimed his model could generate a reliable estimate of risk and overcome the curse of the skew.

How did he do it? He selected certain movie characteristics (such as actor, director, genre, budget, release date, and rating) and estimated which ones would make a winner in the future by analyzing data for the same characteristics from previous films. The model produced a range of potential profits based on how these characteristics had performed in the past. Picking which movies to invest in based on certain factors can mean less risk because the distribution such a strategy produces can offer more reliable risk estimates.

For example, action movies are riskier investments because they are more expensive to make. From 2008 to 2016, the average production budget for an action movie was about $104 million versus a more modest $19 million for the average horror movie. Only about 35 percent of action movies earned back their production costs at the box office compared with 67 percent of horror movies. So Hollywood makes more horror movies, right? Wrong. Between 2007 and 2016, more than two times as many action films than horror films were produced (216 versus 103).

The figure on the following page plots the range of payoffs for both action and horror movies. More action movies get made for many reasons: they tend to do well internationally; they offer the possibility of franchising and merchandising; and because their box office returns are less skewed, their performance is more predictable and they are therefore less risky as investments. Horror movie returns, on the other hand, have a very long tail: many lose money, and there's a wide range of payoffs for the winners. Even if they are profitable more often than action films, they are in some ways riskier because they are less predictable.

Kavanaugh claimed that his model could produce a range of reliable potential earning scenarios, because the process of selecting certain characteristics* enhanced predictability and the odds of earning a profit. And if more than 70 percent of those earning scenarios were associated with enough profit, Kavanaugh told investors to put their money in the film as part of a slate of other movies he handpicked.

---

* Because Relativity favored films with smaller budgets, it usually did not pick action movies in its slate.

Studios were so enthusiastic about the potential for financing that they shared full data on their profits with Kavanaugh; he called it the "Holy Grail" of Hollywood.

The Excel spreadsheet contained the Holy Grail data and transformed it into something even more elusive and desirable: reliable

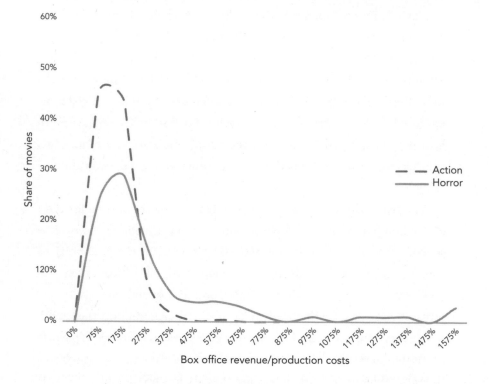

risk estimates that the hedge funds and banks needed to green-light investment. They plowed hundreds of millions of dollars into the movies Kavanaugh picked. In 2005 and 2006, he financed thirty-six movies with Universal and Sony and made money for his investors. Hedge fund investors earned a $150 million profit on one of his early slates, a return of between 13 percent and 18 percent. Kavanaugh was paid millions of dollars per movie and got a producer credit despite having no role in production.

But then Kavanaugh got greedy. Elliott Management, a $21 billion hedge fund, paid $67 million for 49.5 percent of Relativity in 2008. This gave Kavanaugh access to the money he needed to start investing in movies himself. His spending got out of control: his private bathroom had toilet paper with an image of President Obama on it; he brought exotic animals into the office; and he started to work out of a lavishly decorated airport hangar. Even worse, his magic model stopped working, selecting bombs like *The Warrior's Way,* which cost $42 million to make and brought in $5.7 million in the United States, and *Machine Gun Preacher,* with U.S. earnings of only $539,000. Elliott Management pulled out in 2010. Kavanaugh managed to find more financial backers, but he continued to struggle as his spending accelerated and he picked more duds. Relativity was bankrupt by 2016.

Once again, Hollywood broke a risk model.

THE PAST IS A LOUSY WAY TO PREDICT THE FUTURE

Another reason measuring risk in Hollywood is precarious is that the data gets stale fast. Kavanaugh's infamous Monte Carlo simulation predicted the future, but the inputs his model relied on were from the past.

And for a while it worked. Investors got the numbers they needed to feel comfortable, and they made money off their investments. It seemed as though Kavanaugh's simulation did what no other model could do. But that's the thing about predicting the future based on the past. It works until it doesn't, because the market (especially for movies) keeps changing, and estimates based on old data no longer tell you much of anything; what is difficult is knowing when you need to update your data. Often we don't realize the world is changing until long after it has changed.

In the last ten years alone, DVD sales dried up, China became a bigger market, and franchise movies about comic-book characters became more profitable. Streaming and better TVs mean people are less inclined to go to theaters. Online review sites like Rotten Tomatoes can undermine even the best-laid marketing plans. It has led some industry experts, like the *Wall Street Journal* reporter Ben Fritz, to argue that the market has fundamentally changed forever. That would mean data from fifteen years ago tells us nothing about the movie market today. He argues studios will make fewer movies each year going forward and concentrate on films about comic-book characters.

Stale data undermines more than predicting which movies will break box office records. Voting patterns from the Obama/Romney election weren't relevant for making inferences in the Trump/Clinton election, which resulted in misleading poll projections. Technology and more global trade alter old economic relationships and make past data less relevant today.

The JPMorgan media executive David Shaheen described Kavanaugh's model as "garbage in garbage out." He argues that Relativity Media used the wrong data, the wrong way. Maintaining a data set that is accurate and can pick which movies are winners is difficult if not impossible when the data changes so quickly. Shaheen and his colleagues speculate that while comic-book franchise movies look like a sure bet today, the market will eventually become saturated and another fad will come along. Unpredictability means Hollywood quickly latches on to fads one day only to totally abandon them the next.

TERRIBLE IS THE BEST WE'VE GOT, AND IT'S COMING TO A THEATER NEAR YOU

Kavanaugh overpromised because there are no perfect risk estimates. Risk, a measurement of uncertainty, is a human construct that attempts to bring order to an unknowable future. Risk is meant to help us understand what we are up against and plan for what might happen, good or bad. It also helps us weigh different options and see which ones bring us closer to our goals. We use data to make choices every day: trying out a new restaurant because we enjoyed the chef's food before or returning to our favorite resort because we had a great vacation there last year. Sometimes these estimates fall short, because management at the resort changes or the chef's new restaurant is not as good.

Data may be a terrible way to predict the future, but it is the best we've got because it is all we have. The limitations of data are in some ways becoming more apparent in a rapidly changing world that renders past data useless in an instant. At the same time, data is becoming a more powerful tool to measure risk. The modern world is taking the original ideas of Pascal, Fermat, and Bernoulli even further because now we have more and better data, with more computing power to measure risk than ever before. Endless amounts of data exist on what we buy, what we watch, and who we know. We have apps on our phones that can turn this data into predictions about likely flight delays, how well we'll match with a blind date, and stock market ups and downs.

More data and estimation techniques, like machine learning, mean more reliable risk estimates. Soon things that once seemed immeasurable, like the odds a movie will be successful, could be possible.

Netflix can give you a recommendation based on the odds that someone with your demographic profile finished viewing a movie.

Instead of making risky decisions based on a rough estimate from your past moviegoing experience, you can make decisions based on millions of other people's experiences. As Bernoulli showed, more data means more accuracy. That will empower us to make more informed decisions, though we also need to be aware of data's limitations.

A question remains that data cannot answer yet: Does Hollywood make so many bad films because it is so hard to measure risk with changing data and skewed distributions, or does a poorly functioning, undisciplined market in which the biggest risk takers, the people who finance the movies, don't reap the biggest reward but invest anyway because of the glamour, create the skewed distribution?

We'll soon find out.

Technology is again changing the movie market, given the rise of people streaming content in their homes. Amazon and Netflix, which are now in the production business, have data on precisely who watches what and whether they finish. Right now, almost half of a movie's budget is spent on marketing because films are advertised to everyone, with the vague hope the advertising will appeal to someone. Now that studios have data on viewing patterns, they can better tailor their marketing strategy and know which movies will appeal to their intended audience for far less money. This is expected to change the distribution of potential outcomes, narrowing it and making it more predictable.

This might transform the kinds of films that are made, reduce the skew, and maybe even means we'll start seeing better movies.

Chapter 5

DIFFERENT TYPES OF RISK:
The Secret Lives of the Paparazzi

Dream, diversify—and never miss an angle.

—WALT DISNEY

O n Wall Street, people obsess about risk, using high-speed com- puters and advanced math to identify different kinds of it and how to profit off it. But just a few miles away, I found an equally rich investigation of risk in action when I met a New York–based paparazzo whose entire livelihood depends on knowing the kinds of risk he faces. The strategy he uses is a similar, albeit low-tech, version of what fi- nance mavens employ to separate out and manage the kinds of risk he must confront. But his best risk strategy is constantly undermined by an ever-present incentive to cheat.

A ginormous billboard featuring the model Gigi Hadid hangs over a street in one of New York's trendiest neighborhoods. Gigi's image overlooks real-life Gigi's apartment, where she is holed up with her boy- friend. On the street below a handful of middle-aged men gather, each holding a large camera. We discuss Gigi's latest movements. "Yesterday she had dinner with her mother and sister; then Kendall Jenner came over," one of them says. "Now she's up there with Zayn. They've been up there for ages—what do *you* think they are doing?!"

It seems weird that I am discussing a twenty-two-year-old's mundane schedule with grown men. But knowing Gigi's schedule means money for these paparazzi. A simple photo of Gigi leaving her apartment will bring in a relatively small amount of money, maybe $10. But because the people in her life are also famous, getting a picture of them together can be worth hundreds of dollars. And if they do something unusual, it can mean a small fortune. "If someone grabs her, like what happened in Paris, we're talking maybe a hundred thousand dollars," another of the men explains to me.

Getting that special shot of Gigi is unpredictable. Good photography skills certainly help, but often it comes down to luck: standing in exactly the right spot at exactly the right time. It is a risk that can be hard, if not impossible, to control.

Gigi's image is an asset and its value is increasing. Months before, the paparazzi's main focus had been Gigi's friend Kendall Jenner. But one of the photographers tells me that asset had fallen in value: "No more Kendall; now it's Gigi."

THE PAPARAZZI'S GOLDEN RULES

Outside Gigi's apartment I meet Santiago Baez. He's been a paparazzo since the early 1990s. He is a Zelig-like character in New York's recent cultural history. Camera in hand, he's witnessed the fallout of extramarital affairs, new babies, deaths, new love, and breakups of some of New York's most famous residents. And he's invested. We stand outside the apartment where Naomi Watts and Liev Schreiber once lived together and when I ask about their breakup, he laments, "That was rough. I was very upset about that one. I followed them for years. They are nice people, a good family."

A few days after meeting outside Gigi's apartment, we reconnect to find Alec Baldwin and his wife, Hilaria. Baez had a tip they were leaving for the Hamptons and planning on renewing their wedding vows. As Baez explained, a newsworthy photo of a celebrity is more lucrative than a shot of a star going out for a stroll.

Baez's much younger wife, whose name I was never told (Baez calls her "the good wife"), is his photography partner. She is there too, along with their son in a stroller. As we begin to camp outside Baldwin's apartment, a woman rushes out of an ice cream store with a cone for Baez's son. Baez explains it is important to build relationships with the people who work in businesses near celebrities' homes because they'll let you use their restroom. The paparazzi might spend several hours waiting for their shot, sometimes weeks.

Baez came to New York in 1981 from the Dominican Republic. He worked in leather production and as a busboy. He taught himself English by using a dictionary and reading the newspaper. Money was tight, but one of the first things he bought was a $300 camera on layaway. He always wanted to be an architect, but "it was too much money" to study, so he pursued photography instead. When he was just a busboy who didn't know English, he remembers telling his barber that "one day I'll be a professional photographer. He thought I was crazy."

After a few years, Baez got a better-paying job. In the meantime, he started going to red-carpet events with his camera to take pictures and sell them to local papers. Then in 1991, outside an awards event, Baez met an older French paparazzo who had made a small fortune selling salacious photos of Sarah Ferguson, the Duchess of York. He told Baez that he should quit his day job to be a full-time paparazzo. The older photographer took Baez under his wing, introducing him to his photo agency and the intermediary who sold photographs to the glossy magazines. He schooled Baez in the craft, teaching him where to stand, how to aim his camera, how to hide, what lenses to use, and the golden rules of celebrity photography: (1) don't let them see you and (2) if they do see you, don't talk to them unless they speak to you first.

Outside Baldwin's apartment Baez shows me some of these skills in action—the exact spot to stand if Baldwin exits his apartment and the right angle to hold the camera. We set up for the first rule of paparazzi photography, looking for places to hide behind a garbage can or around the corner, since we didn't want Baldwin to see us. Once a celebrity looks at the camera, it shatters the illusion. The best pictures are the ones celebrities don't know are being taken. The shot must be unobstructed, show Baldwin's face, and not include other people. We might only have seconds to get that perfect picture.

Paired with an encyclopedic knowledge of where famous people live in New York, Baez has a network of drivers and shop and restaurant workers who will call and tip him off when celebrities are in the vicinity. Often the tips are from the celebrities themselves via social media: looking to build a following, they alert the public (mostly directed at photographers) about their movements. At other times, Baez's photo agency tells him to be somewhere. If a celebrity wants to be photographed, his or her publicist will call an agency and they will dispatch Baez.

Some photographers specialize in certain celebrities. For example, Baez used to follow Isabella Rossellini and John F. Kennedy Jr. in the 1990s. Specializing can be a good strategy because you learn your subject's schedule, which increases the odds of getting the right shot. You can also manage the supply of pictures of that celebrity and not flood the market. But the market for a certain celebrity's pictures can disappear, as it did for Paris Hilton, and with it, the value of knowing her schedule.

Most pictures aren't worth much, but that great shot of a new baby, a celebrity kissing a new paramour, or a wedding can change fortunes on a dime. And that mostly comes down to being in the right place at the right time. The element of luck and timing means a paparazzo's income is extremely risky, because it is so variable and unpredictable. They face the risk that one day they won't get any pictures at all and on another they might stumble upon a celebrity eating breakfast with a new lover. The paparazzi have various ways of managing these risks, but even the best strategies are undermined by infighting and a changing industry.

Since the best shots come down to being in the right place at the right time, photogs often form teams or alliances to share tips and sometimes royalties to increase the odds or payoffs they'll be in that place. In 2003, Baez founded a group called PACO, "like the jeans," combining the words "paparazzi" and "company."

PACO consisted of ten experienced photographers. They traded tips on where certain celebrities hung out and when. So if Baez spotted a celebrity eating lunch at a trendy restaurant, he would alert the other PACO members. He says, beaming with pride, "Back in the day when we'd show up, the other guys would say, 'Oh no, here comes PACO,' because we were the *best*."

But the temptation to cheat on the alliance, to withhold an especially good tip or not share the money evenly, means any alliance is as fragile as a celebrity marriage. After all, getting a picture no one else has means more money. If a paparazzo is the only one who gets that life-changing shot, he or she has every incentive to cheat on the alliance, which in turn leads to bitterness among the photographers. PACO* lasted ten years, a lifetime in the celebrity photography world.

"Celebrity photographers have no loyalty," Baez complains, still disappointed by how many friendships ended over cheating on an alliance.

Infighting and an incentive to cheat undermine the paparazzi's ability to reduce the risk of narrowly missing the right shot and increase

---

* Last I heard, the current powerful alliance, which Baez was not part of, is called the Bowery Boys, because they spend lots of time in front of New York City's Bowery Hotel (no relation to the nineteenth-century nativist gang or the film actors of the 1940s and '50s).

the odds of stumbling on the right one. And more recently they face a different risk, one that is even harder to manage.

THE PAPARAZZI GOLD RUSH

The price of paparazzi photographs is determined by a handful of people like Peter Grossman, the photo editor at *Us Weekly* from 2003 to 2017. Grossman didn't work with paparazzi directly; instead, a photographer like Baez sells his pictures to an agency that has the relationship with photo editors like Grossman.* A paparazzo receives anywhere between 20 percent and 70 percent of the royalties the picture earns, depending on the photographer and the deal he or she negotiated with the agency. The more senior, skilled, and talented paparazzi command better terms, which often includes exclusively selling their pictures to just one agency. But this exclusivity is often broken by paparazzi who cheat by selling photos under different names.

Grossman and I met up a few times to discuss the business in a small Brooklyn restaurant. Our conversations often veered off topic; I could not get enough of his gossipy stories from his years on the front lines, though the economics behind celebrity pictures is just as interesting.

Grossman told me one of his biggest hits was a series of photographs of the actress Kristen Stewart, who was dating the actor Robert Pattinson at the time, in a passionate embrace with Rupert Sanders, the married director of *Snow White and the Huntsman*, a film she had starred in. One day in 2012, a group of paparazzi snapped her leaving her gym in Los Angeles; these were standard pictures not worth much. They all left as she got in her car, but one photog decided to follow her. He noticed that instead of driving home, she turned in to a parking lot and met up with a man who was not her boyfriend. The photographer

---

* Relationships with the agencies are critical; even in an age when everyone has a phone camera, paparazzi are the only ones who can sell pictures, because of their relationships with agencies.

knew he struck gold as he snapped the pictures. His agent was so excited that he woke Grossman in the middle of the night. He called to tell him he had the biggest gets of his career. Grossman says he paid "mid six figures" for them. Pictures like them only come along "once in a generation."

Grossman was the man behind the rise of "Just Like Us" pictures. On April 1, 2002, *Us Weekly* first published its "Stars—They're Just Like Us!" weekly series featuring pictures of celebrities doing mundane tasks like getting coffee or pumping gas. Before this, everyday pictures were not worth much, but *Us Weekly* humanized celebrities by showing them looking less glamorous. People loved it, and soon lots of outlets were publishing these types of pictures, kicking off what's known in the industry as the gold rush years, coinciding with the heyday of Paris Hilton, Britney Spears, and Lindsay Lohan.

Grossman described that back in the gold rush days, the price he'd pay for a photograph depended on what the celebrity was doing and whether it was an "exclusive," the only shot of a celebrity doing a particular activity. At the gold rush peak, an exclusive "Just Like Us" picture would typically fetch $5,000 to $15,000.

The gold rush era brought about gold rush mentality, with many new photographers flocking to the industry, willing to break laws and giving paparazzi a still worse reputation for going too far and harassing celebrities and even their young children. Grossman had had enough. He convened a dinner straight out of *The Godfather,* only instead of the bosses of crime families, he invited top editors, heads of photo agencies, and the best photographers. He urged everyone to take a coordinated step back, pay less for pictures, and not break laws or put themselves or others in danger to get the shot. It didn't work. Because cooperation always fails in the celebrity photo business, it undermines the industry's risk reduction.

The Great Recession and the rise of online media finally killed the gold rush. Digital media increased the demand for celebrity photographs but decreased the price media companies were willing to pay for them. Photo agencies began to consolidate or go out of business, and the remaining ones changed their business model. Instead of making magazines pay per photo, they offered a subscription service: publishers could use as many photos as they wanted to fulfill the greater demand for cheaper shots. As a result, paparazzi are paid a small fraction of the subscription fee; how much depends on how many of their pictures are used each month. That means an exclusive "Just Like Us" photo, which would have fetched $5,000 to $15,000 before, now pays only $5 or $10.

The life of a paparazzo is hard and getting harder. Gone are the days when many paparazzi could count on a six-figure income. Now getting that white whale—another Kristen Stewart affair picture—is necessary to earn big money.

IDIOSYNCRATIC VERSUS SYSTEMATIC RISK

I must admit that stalking celebrities with the paparazzi was tremendous fun. I went out with Baez a few times. He would give me little jobs to do: staking out a corner to see who was coming or providing cover when he took a picture of a starlet. I felt like a spy on a mission. There was a rush when we'd see a celebrity because often it happened by chance, which is exactly part of the reason why Baez's income is so volatile. Not surprisingly, Baez employs risk strategies in his craft similar to what people use in financial markets.

Financial economists separate risk into two broad categories: the first is idiosyncratic risk, or the risk unique to a particular asset. Suppose Facebook changes management; the future of the company is unclear, and the price of the stock might drop based on factors unique to Facebook that don't impact any other stock.

The paparazzi face lots of idiosyncratic risk. What Gigi does today—whether she spends time with her A-list or D-list friends, whether the paparazzi can catch her if she leaves a restaurant by the back or front door, or whether she wears a little black dress or sweats—determines how much they earn that week. If Gigi stops being interesting or popular, the value of these pictures decreases. Images of Gigi are like a stock: their value varies based on factors unique to Gigi and a particular photographer getting the right shot at the right time.

The second kind of risk is systematic risk, or risk that affects the larger system instead of an individual asset. Systematic risk is when every stock rises or falls together because the entire market surges or crashes, as it did in 2008. Systematic risk events often happen because of a big economic disruption like a recession or an election result that people think will impact business. Systematic risks are harder to manage than idiosyncratic risks, and the downsides are potentially more dangerous. If the entire stock market tanks, you risk losing your job and stock portfolio at the same time.

You can see systematic risk play out with paparazzi, like the boom of the gold rush years and the crash when people stopped buying $5 tabloids during the recession. The downside of systematic paparazzi risk has become more severe in the last ten years. It is harder for everyone to make money. Many paparazzi have left the business. After nearly thirty years of taking celebrity photographs, Baez sadly moved back to the Dominican Republic in the summer of 2018, with his wife and son, to find new work.

In fact, paparazzi experience both types of risk in higher degrees than most people do in their jobs. They are an extreme example, but that's why they offer a valuable illustration of how to spot idiosyncratic and systematic risks and try to manage them. All of us must deal with different kinds of risk in our jobs, our relationships, even our choices of where we eat.

Suppose you decide to try the new local sushi restaurant. The idiosyncratic risk is that this particular restaurant has bad fish that will make you sick. The systematic risk is a widespread parasite infecting tuna everywhere.

Being able to spot the difference is important because it determines what the best risk strategy is (we'll cover this topic in later chapters). For example, when you are looking to buy a house, the price might be driven by idiosyncratic risk (a new trendy feature like concrete countertops in the kitchen) or systematic risk (the whole market is hot and driving up prices). Discerning different types of risk can tell you if you are overpaying or if now is the right time to buy.

IT PAYS TO KNOW THE DIFFERENCE

The way to manage idiosyncratic risk in finance is to buy lots of stocks. Owning the stocks of many companies means you'll barely notice when one corporation whose stock you own goes bankrupt because of bad management since your risk is spread out among many companies. You shouldn't own stock in the company you work for because you're exposed to a great deal of your employer's idiosyncratic risk. For example, if you had worked at Enron and owned stock, you would have lost your job, your income, and your retirement savings all in one fell swoop when a major accounting scandal led to its insolvency.

The paparazzi also manage their idiosyncratic risk by spreading it around. This is what they are doing when they form an alliance or work in teams. Each photographer bears lots of risk based on how lucky he is that day: if he catches a celebrity with her latest paramour in public; if the celebrity leaves a trendy restaurant through the back door where the photographer happens to be standing. A paparazzi alliance pools their luck, reducing their idiosyncratic risk. This means more stable income because it increases the odds of getting the right shot. However, the incentive to cheat constantly undermines a paparazzo's ability to reduce idiosyncratic risk. Baez spent his career constantly forming new alliances, knowing he'd eventually get burned, because it was the only way to reduce the tremendous idiosyncratic risk he faced. It was worth it.

Systematic risk is even harder to manage. To measure systematic risk, finance professionals look at the history of stock prices and see how much one stock price moves with the rest of the market. That produces a single number, based on this correlation, called market beta.

In the 1960s, the economists William Sharpe and John Lintner developed a theory that market beta can explain why one stock returns more than another. Idiosyncratic risk can be reduced easily by owning lots of different stocks—any other stock. But a stock that reduces systematic risk is especially valuable, because it is more rare and has the power to reduce risk for your entire portfolio. A stock that moves in a different direction or less strongly than the rest of the market has a low beta, which reduces your systematic risk and makes you safer, so it offers a lower expected return. Conversely, a stock sensitive to the rest of the market, one that goes up 15 percent when the rest of the market only goes up 5 percent, has a high beta. It amplifies systematic risk in your investment portfolio, so you'd only want to buy that stock if you are compensated for taking on more risk. It should promise you a much higher return. If you want to reduce risk in your portfolio, you need lower-beta stocks; if you want higher returns and are comfortable with lots of non-diversifiable risk, you want high-beta stocks.

Our lives are full of high-beta risky decisions. Imagine you are deciding the fastest way to get home and can take either a back road or a major highway. A back road poses the idiosyncratic risk that you'll get stuck behind a slow car. The major highway is probably faster, but it has more systematic risk because during busy times, like rush hour, you'll encounter traffic. Or say you are offered a job in construction; it has a high beta because construction jobs pay off when the economy is booming, but workers in the industry are the first to lose their jobs when there's a recession.

The payoffs for "Stars—They're Just Like Us!" pictures pose more systematic risk because they are especially sensitive to the market. When the market for celebrity pictures was booming, media outlets were willing to pay thousands of dollars for these kinds of photos. But their value plunged to only a few dollars after the market crashed during the recession and digital media surpassed print. And yet these pictures are still popular because they are relatively cheap and easy to obtain since most of the time celebrities are actually just like us. The relative return, for time and effort, on these photos is high compared with that of other kinds of pictures with less market sensitivity.

For example, an exclusive baby picture pays off in any market, but it can take weeks of time and effort to get a good one. (Baez told me he sometimes had to dedicate as much as two solid weeks for the perfect shot.) Just like a fund manager, a paparazzo must balance his objectives and risk tolerance to decide what photos are worth the investment of his time.

THE PAPARAZZI ARE JUST LIKE US TOO

The job of a paparazzo is riskier than most. But to some extent we all face some level of idiosyncratic and systematic risk in our careers, so we can learn a lot from these photogs.

Suppose you want to change jobs from a safe, salaried support role to a sales job based on commission. Odds are you'll earn more than you did in the salaried job because as a salesperson you will face both kinds of risk: It is a high-beta job with loads of idiosyncratic risk; for example, how much you earn will depend on your sales skills and the behavior of your clients (you can manage this risk by working in a team and having lots of clients). You will also face systematic risk because sales depend on the state of the economy.

Systematic risk is especially dangerous. In an economic downturn, your pay may be reduced or disappear entirely, it is likely to be harder to find another job, your assets might take a hit, and your partner's income may be at risk too. The more systematic risk associated with your job, the more exposed you are.

To find out which Americans face the greatest systematic income risk, economists measured trends in American earnings when the economy was up or down since the 1950s using Social Security records. They noticed a U-shaped pattern with income and systematic risk, which indicates that systematic risk is more severe for both very low-paid and very high-paid workers, while people in the middle face less risk.

It is not surprising that the lowest earners are also the most vulnerable when the economy falters. They work in industries with high betas, like retail, that tend to crash when the economy goes south. As a general rule, the more you earn, the safer you are.

But there is an exception: when it comes to the highest earners, the relationship changes. For example, people who work in finance make ridiculous amounts of money, but they also often expect to lose their jobs when the economy sours (the more systematic risk you take on, the bigger your expected gains). Of course, few people feel sorry for them. Their income is so high, they can survive a layoff better than minimum-wage employees who live paycheck to paycheck and also risk being laid off in a downturn. But at least some of the high pay in the finance industry is compensation for the fact that the income of its workers is more sensitive to economic conditions.

If you take a job in the government, your income has a low beta; it is fairly stable, no matter what the state of the economy is. High-skilled people who work in government are often paid less than their private sector counterparts in exchange for assuming less systematic income risk.

From one perspective, you can look at economic data and conclude that the job market is less risky for most Americans. In the 1980s, more than 25 percent of American workers had been in their job for less than one year. That figure hovers around 20 percent today, even in a tight job market. It could be that we stay in jobs a little longer because technology makes it easier to find the right fit and reduce the idiosyncratic risk a job won't work out. But from the perspective of systematic risk, we face graver job risks that are harder to manage.

WHY WE FEEL SO MUCH ECONOMIC ANXIETY

The livelihood of the average paparazzo is threatened by major changes in the publication industry. The photogs manage idiosyncratic risk by forming unstable alliances, but the larger systematic risk that could wipe out their jobs is harder to manage. They could form a union and demand better terms from the agencies, but historically they struggle to cooperate with one another. And the paparazzi are not the only ones who face the risk that their jobs will no longer be viable.

One reason people seem to worry more about their economic future than they did in the past is that they sense more systematic risk in the job market. A few decades ago, most of the employment risk was idiosyncratic: conflict with the boss, a position that was a bad fit, a poorly managed company. If you lost your job, you could probably find another one just like it. Workers formed trade unions, banded together, and demanded better pay and benefits, confident that there was a need for their skills. The job market had its ups and downs, but risk seemed to be relatively easy to manage.

In today's economy, systematic risk is more acute. There's a chance technology—robots and artificial intelligence—could take over your job or at least require new skills you don't have. If you lose your job during a recession, you may never find a similar one.

What is happening to the paparazzi is part of a larger trend that threatens everyone.

B aez and I spent hours searching for the Baldwins. We never found them; the tips were no good and the couple had already left for the Hamptons. This is the way of life for paparazzi: hours of work and no photos to sell. It is a risky business that is only getting riskier with fewer rewards.

I can understand why Baez loved the work and was sad to leave it. It is hard to describe the exhilaration you feel after waiting for hours to see a celebrity emerge, slender and glamorous, wearing huge sunglasses and a track suit, greeted by the flash of camera lights. The paparazzi spy her and gasp with excitement. You can almost see the adrenaline fueling their steps as they follow Gigi down the sidewalk, smiles of satisfaction barely visible under the large cameras that just about cover their faces.

RULE 2

I AM IRRATIONAL AND I KNOW IT

We want to think we're rational beings. And for the most part, we are. But perhaps the most obvious place to witness our irrationality at work is when we make a risky decision. This is when human nature gets in the way, and sometimes we make choices we later regret. Don't fear: you can learn about the underpinnings of irrationality at work, what's likely to trigger it, and how to avoid these traps to make better decisions more often.

Our feelings about losses versus gains can lead us to make decisions economists think are irrational. For example, if we are gambling and losing, we should just walk away, but our reluctance to accept loss means we keep playing. People who make bets every day, professional gamblers and traders, have learned to overcome their aversion to loss; in chapter 6 we'll explore what they do.

In chapter 7 we'll examine how we perceive risk. We're rarely moved by just cold, rational data alone. Risk perception comes down to how the data is presented to us. This can have an enormous amount of sway over the decisions we make, and it gives merchants and policy makers power over how we behave and take risks. Understanding a different way to make sense of risk gives us more power in any economic transaction.

By knowing yourself, how to gauge risk, and your natural response to potentially losing, you can make better risky decisions.

Chapter 6

PROSPECT THEORY:
Tilting Toward Rationality

Victory is fleeting. Losing is forever.

—BILLIE JEAN KING

No one likes to lose. It feels terrible. When we face a risky situation, the desire to avoid loss can lead us astray from what financial economics predicts we should do. And this behavior sometimes means we make decisions we regret and lose even more. But if we go into a risky situation armed with more knowledge and experience, we can improve our behavior, even if we still hate to lose.

Take professional poker player Phil Hellmuth. His success depends on overcoming his emotions. He has spent years learning certain tricks to control his behavior. When it counts, he has learned to stay rational and in control, and then he explodes....

Professional etiquette usually dictates a certain measure of civility. In competitive fields, it requires being a gracious loser. Losing is hard, especially when adrenaline is flowing, yet we must grit our teeth, shake our adversary's hand, and congratulate them on a hard-won victory.

Phil Hellmuth has no patience for such niceties. When he loses a poker tournament, he throws a tantrum. He gets up from the table, paces, yells expletives, and insults the winner's intelligence (especially when his opponent is an amateur). To be fair, he reserves the harshest criticism for himself. As he paces he mutters to himself, reliving every hand, what he played, what he let go, and how he could have done better against the idiot "who can't even spell poker!"

Hellmuth owns it—he even titled his autobiography *Poker Brat,* after his industry nickname. You can check out a montage of his meltdowns on YouTube. One of his most notorious tantrums followed a close loss to Annie Duke at the 2004 Tournament of Champions, an invite-only World Series of Poker event for the top ten players, with the winner poised to take home $2 million (but no money for second place). After knocking out the other players, Hellmuth and Duke cut a deal behind the scenes—each would take home $750,000, so they were guaranteed something. They returned to the table to play for the $500,000 still up for grabs. Duke prevailed, and Hellmuth went nuts, pacing and yelling expletives. He recalls his tantrum in *Poker Brat,* admitting it was different from his other fits:

> I lurched into the only time in my life when I acted for the cameras. Sadly, all the other outbursts, the ones that have tens of millions of hits on YouTube, are me genuinely losing control. Don't get me wrong, I was smoking hot mad after I busted, but the $750,000 save had softened the blow. In any case, I exaggerated my usual tantrum, and it did make for good television. Harrah's appreciated my tantrum, and so did ESPN, because ratings for the 2004 TOC were off the hook!

Hellmuth says he has ADHD; he struggles to maintain focus and is emotional. In my conversations with him I found him short-tempered and quick to express his frustration with me, which are not generally helpful qualities for a poker player.

Hellmuth tells me that he knows the key to good play is patience and control, but his interpretation of this is different from what you might expect. He explains a highly disciplined style of play to me: "Playing good poker means only playing 12 percent of your hands. You can't make money if you play more than 30 percent, and if you play 100 percent you'll go broke every day."

Research from online poker games estimates that most people play way more hands than Hellmuth, between 25 percent and 50 percent of the hands they are dealt. Hellmuth's success comes from his ability to overcome his emotions, called tilt in the poker world, and choose the right hands to play.

Great poker players are not only patient but also calm, collected, and aware of others around them and how they process information. Given Hellmuth's volatile nature, it is remarkable that he is considered one of the world's best players. He won fifteen World Series of Poker gold bracelets, a record number of wins, and he tells me he's worth more than $20 million.

YOU CAN'T SPELL HELLMUTH WITHOUT HELL

In 1986, Hellmuth called his parents in Madison, Wisconsin, to announce he was dropping out of college to play poker professionally. His multidegreed academic father was less than thrilled. And Hellmuth's career did not get off to an auspicious start, when only five months later, with just 47 cents in his pocket, he called his parents collect from Vegas to beg them for money to fly home. His father almost didn't take the call, and finally his mother gave him the money, making it clear it would be the last time.

Just three years later, as his father looked on, Hellmuth stared down the Fila jumpsuit–clad reigning poker champion, Johnny Chan, and won his first World Series of Poker in a game of no-limit Texas hold 'em.

The world of professional poker is a unique subculture—complete with special outfits and lingo—that appears foreign to outsiders. Its obsessive fan base watches games on television or in person for hours, is preoccupied with stats, and gambles on the players and games. Winning at poker comes down to luck and skill. Luck is being dealt a winning hand. Skill is knowing how and when to bet, and having the discipline and ability to infer what other players are doing.

Hellmuth realized early that he had to overcome his natural tendencies in order to succeed: "I guess what it all meant was that I needed to have the discipline of a monk if I was to succeed in poker. I needed to exercise patience relentlessly and to allow no negative emotion to affect my mood."

He took the monk part literally, and in the years leading up to his first World Series win, he didn't drink and was celibate. Getting his emotions in check was a constant battle. He'd sometimes play impulsively, was cheated, and would berate himself for any mistakes he made. He also experienced huge swings in his wealth, winning hundreds of thousands of dollars at one tournament and losing almost all of it at the next.

Keeping control of his emotions was all-consuming; he even passed out from exhaustion during an early poker tournament. While self-control is an ongoing struggle for Hellmuth, he admits that over the years it's gotten easier to check his impulses. He still loses his cool sometimes but has willed himself to be the master of risk taking under pressure. Behind the scenes a thoughtful strategy is at work: Hellmuth not only overcomes his own behavioral quirks but channels them into a winning brand.

WHY WE HATE TO LOSE

Hellmuth is an extreme case in both temperament and career choice. But if he can pull it off, then anyone should be able to, because he, like all of us, is prone to common behaviors when faced with risk.

If we let our emotions influence our decision making when risk is involved (and we all do), then we may not accurately measure the risks we face or we may plow ahead without a clear goal. But even when we have a firm grasp on our goal and all the risks are clearly presented to us, we still make choices that don't appear to be in our best interest.

When we calculate risk, the rational way to estimate it is to think through all possibilities and weight them by how probable they are. If the odds add up to something we want, it is a risk worth taking. But we aren't cold, rational number crunchers. We put some emotional value on certain things happening.

Suppose you are deciding whether or not to go on a date with someone you met on Tinder. Based on your extensive dating experience, you figure there's a 5 percent chance the date will be a total bust. You will spend the whole time being lectured about some politically motivated conspiracy theory, alternating with subtle put-downs about your age and appearance. There is a 60 percent chance your date will be perfectly nice, but there will be no chemistry and awkward, strained conversation. There is a 30 percent chance you'll like each other enough to date for three months and then break up and feel indifferent about it. And there's a 5 percent chance the date will be amazing and you'll walk away thinking you met the love of your life.

Deciding whether or not to go on the date isn't just a matter of 35 percent good versus 65 percent bad. If you look at it that way, you'll never leave home.

We have strong emotions attached to each potential outcome. How we feel about, or value, each possibility is what economists call utility.

The prospect of a good relationship gives us so much joy, or lots of utility, we are willing to go on what will probably be a bad date.

In the date example, optimism gets us off the sofa. We are willing to risk worse than even odds to find love. But when it comes to most decisions in life, we often put more weight on the bad outcomes.

The eighteenth-century scientist Daniel Bernoulli (the nephew of Jakob Bernoulli from chapter 4—the Bernoullis were a very impressive and competitive family!) made the observation that when we make a risky decision and weigh the different possibilities, how we feel about each outcome, not just its value (even if it is money), is what matters. In most situations, economists, like Bernoulli, assume we place less value on money as we get more of it. One thousand dollars is nothing to a millionaire, but it is serious money for someone on welfare. This diminishing utility of money explains why people are risk averse. They prefer certainty to a risk.

Suppose you were offered a gamble:

A: $45 for certain, or

B: a 50 percent chance of $100 or a 50 percent chance of nothing

If emotions did not enter into the equation, the expected outcome from a bet is:

A = $45

B = 0.5 * $100 + 0.5 * 0 = $50

Taking the risk will pay off most of the time. But economists assume that when you factor in the value people place on each incremental dollar value, the certain outcome is more appealing, and most people will take the $45. We'll take less money if we can be guaranteed certainty over risk because we are risk averse.

Risk aversion is why lower-risk assets offer lower returns. Riskier assets offer the possibility of higher payoffs because investors need to be compensated for the risk they are taking on. It is why a simple no-risk bank account pays almost no interest, but a mutual fund made up of many stocks typically returns an extra 5 percent a year.

Economists assume we are risk-averse and not just with money but with most things in life. We leave early for the airport; we don't let our children walk home alone from school; we may prefer a steady job at an established company to working at a start-up. Economists also assume that we are consistent with risk aversion, and that we always prefer certainty to a gamble.*

But that's not the whole story. Sometimes we make decisions that conflict with this simple narrative. In the twentieth century, two psychologists, Amos Tversky and Daniel Kahneman, shook up both economics and psychology when they introduced prospect theory. Prospect theory says when we weigh different options, the value we place on them depends on how much money we have when we start and if there is the possibility of loss. Humans aren't just risk averse; they hate losing anything—from a $20 bill to a free T-shirt.

Here's another example: Amateur poker player Bob's total wealth is $1 million. Phil's total wealth is $10 million. Both are offered a gamble that changes the value of their net worth:

A: a 50 percent chance to end up with $1 million or a 50 percent
    chance to end up with $10 million, or
B: end up with $5 million for sure

Kahneman and Tversky argue that Bob will happily take option B because there's

---

* Assuming that the two options offer similar expected payouts.

A: a 50 percent chance Bob gets nothing, and a 50 percent chance
   of increasing his wealth tenfold, or

B: a 100 percent chance of increasing his wealth fivefold

Just like Bernoulli predicted, the incremental value of another $5 million once Bob already has $5 million isn't worth taking the risk; he is risk averse to this menu of possible gains.

But when Phil, who has ten times what Bob has, is offered the same bet, he views it differently. From Phil's perspective, his options are

A: a 50 percent chance of losing $9 million and a 50 percent chance
   of losing nothing, or

B: a 100 percent chance of losing half his net worth

Faced with the possibility of certain loss or a 50 percent chance of losing nothing, Phil will take the risky bet. Prospect theory argues that humans are risk seeking, or willing to take a chance on even bigger losses and forgo certainty when offered a menu of loss scenarios.

Before prospect theory, economists assumed we were risk averse all the time. But in this case, Bob is risk averse because he only has money to gain, and Phil is risk seeking because most of his choices involve losing and none involve gaining. Reference points, or how much we have to start with, determine how we view risky choices and what we're likely to do.

It is hard to say whether the behavior prospect theory predicts always results in bad decisions. An outcome that's different from what classical economists predict is not necessarily good or bad. You can think of scenarios in which viewing risk based on your reference point makes sense. I don't know what it would be like to lose $5 million and only have $5 million left. But I can imagine it would cause Phil lots of anxiety and a major change in lifestyle. He surely feels worse about having $5 million than Bob does. Even classical economics assumes it is worse to have been rich and lost it, than never to have been rich at all.

One extension of loss aversion that often results in needless risk taking and more loss than we'd normally tolerate is called the break-even effect. It was first identified by the behavioral economists Richard Thaler and Eric Johnson, who argue that when we lose money and have a chance to win it back right away, or even come out ahead, not only do we take more risk, but we take even bigger risks and thereby subject ourselves to even bigger losses. If we want to avoid loss, it would be better to just walk away. The break-even effect explains your conviction that the next hand of blackjack or the next coin in the slot machine will make you whole or win back your money and then some.

Suppose you are playing a single hand of poker and have $500 to spend. After you see your cards you must decide whether or not to bet your $500 for an $800 pot of money, or walk away from the game. If you think there's a 50 percent probability of winning the $800 and a 50 percent probability of losing your $500, odds are you'll sit the hand out because, as prospect theory predicts, losing $500 feels much worse than the joy of winning $800.

But if you were offered that same bet and had just lost $500 in the previous round, the break-even effect predicts you'll take the bet. Now the bet is between winning back what you lost (plus $300), or losing even more—$1,000. The theory predicts you become less sensitive to incremental losses after losing big.

BREAK-EVEN EFFECT AT WORK: THE WORLD OF ONLINE POKER

Now Phil Hellmuth's conservative approach to which hands to play might seem revolutionary. He developed his philosophy after seeing how often the break-even effect destroyed players in high-stakes poker. "Generally, it is human nature when losing to not want to quit and gamble a little bit more on that particular session," he tells me. "Lots of great pros gamble a bit when they are down and play hands they shouldn't, [thinking] they can climb out [if they] rely on [their] skills. Maybe it works thirty percent of the time."

Hellmuth sees players get lucky when they play aggressively, which leads them to believe if they play this way when they are down they will win their money back. Most of the time, 70 percent by his estimation, it doesn't work out—they lose even more. Hellmuth credits his success with not falling into this trap.

Economists at Pomona College noticed the same thing after studying behavior in an online poker room, where gamers play Texas hold 'em. They recorded what happened in more than 500,000 hands with 1,609 players from January to May 2008. They looked at cases when players won or lost $1,000 and how they played the next twelve hands.

The economists estimated that after a loss about two-thirds of players are looser, more likely to bet to stay in a game than after a loss. The pattern held across all table sizes. The results were even stronger when it came to aggressiveness, or how often a player raises a bid. Most played more aggressively after a loss.

A later study of online poker gamers found similar results. Players were observed taking bigger risks when they were down and playing tighter, or betting less than 20 percent of the time, when they were up. The researchers also noticed that more experienced gamers, like Hellmuth (who only plays 12 percent of the time), were able to overcome this pattern and play consistently, whether up or down.

DOES IT MATTER IF WE ARE IRRATIONAL?

A bond trader at the Chicago Board of Trade who had a morning loss is 15.5 percent more likely to take greater risk in the afternoon compared with a trader who had a morning gain. While it is possible for over-aggressive trading to have some impact on market prices, more rational trading by unbiased traders bid away any price discrepancies at the end of the day.

But other finance examples show that prospect theory can some-times impact the market—just think of how people are less likely to sell a stock that is down than a stock that is up. A winner is more likely to keep going up, but our distaste of experiencing loss means we are more likely to sell a winner than a loser.

Humans make inconsistent risk choices; all economists agree on this, but many aren't convinced it actually shows up in stock prices or has a meaningful impact in markets. After all, surely someone would find it profitable to curb his or her biases and take advantage of every-one else, as Hellmuth does in poker. And now that more trading is driven by computer programs, which aren't so emotional, markets may be more rational than ever.

Is assuming people are rational about taking risks a harmless, sim-plifying assumption or a major blind spot? The debate rages on among academics, and because each thesis is hard to prove definitively, the argument will probably never be resolved. One thing everyone agrees on is that more awareness and education can change our behavior and em-power us to make better risky decisions.

Studies reveal that people who have more experience making risky decisions, like Phil Hellmuth, are less prone to loss avoidance. Experience and education can transform how we take risks. The more we see and deal with risk, the better we get at handling it. But our natural biases are always present. Overcoming them sometimes just comes down to self-control.

HOW TO TAKE RISKS LIKE A POKER CHAMPION

To be successful at poker or in any risky situation, you must not get too emotional or aggressive when losing. You might develop rules for yourself to avoid this behavior; for example, promise yourself that you'll walk away from a bet when you're down $100. But realize that it's hard to stick with these rules when emotions are riding high, and the next hand can win back everything you've lost.

You can also hone the skills you need so that when it really matters you stay calm and wait for the right hand. This is how Phil Hellmuth, notorious for his meltdowns, has managed to become a poker champion. Even after thirty years of playing professional poker, Hellmuth still struggles with his tilt. Here are the strategies he uses to keep his emotions in check to make the best decisions possible to increase the odds of a winning hand.

Never Have Too Much of Your Own Money at Stake

Hellmuth has a firm rule that whenever he goes into a tournament, his own personal stake never exceeds $10,000. He often participates in high-stakes poker tournaments where the minimum buy-in is tens of thousands of dollars. He learned the hard way in his twenties, when he would begin with good intentions of limiting his bankroll (his budget for gambling) but then lose and end up betting more than he planned on, thinking he could win his way back.

Despite these bad habits, Hellmuth had gotten rich by the time he was in his thirties. He started to notice other players his age hit a wall—they had the skills to win but were overconfident and lost overall. Hellmuth resolved that once his net worth fell to $1 million, he'd limit the amount he could possibly lose. From then on, he went into large tournaments "staked" (when outside investors put up money for you to play and then get a share of your winnings).

This means Hellmuth can still win big without ever having to lose too much. Staking also keeps him from getting too desperate when he's down because the worst that can happen is he loses a small fraction of his net worth. When asked about how limiting his exposure keeps him from taking on too much risk, Hellmuth says, "I never have a horrible day—I am already aggravated and pissed off because I hate losing." He exemplifies an extreme version of the rest of us.

Most of us do not know anyone who will subsidize our bets. But there is a lesson to learn from Hellmuth. He gives up some of his potential winnings to avoid having too much on the line that he can lose. We can all do this by tempering the risks we take, otherwise known as hedging (explained in more detail in chapter 9). It might be balancing a stock portfolio with bonds or not taking a bigger salary instead of stock options at work. The principle is the same: when you have less at stake to lose, you stay more rational.

Eliminate Extreme Downside Risk

Hellmuth's autobiography describes, in painstaking detail, every hand in every major poker game he's been in. What sticks out to a less enthusiastic poker fan are the side deals he makes with the other players. At a crucial part of the game, he and the other player often take a break, remove their microphones, and step outside. There, they agree to split the prize money and still offer the winner some extra upside, just as he and Annie Duke did at the 2004 Tournament of Champions.

Having a guaranteed payday (win or lose), in addition to being staked to begin with, helps Hellmuth stay focused; he doesn't panic or play too aggressively, because he is not facing a big loss.

In everyday life we can follow Hellmuth's example by buying insurance. The benefits of insurance are explained in chapter 10. Hellmuth is essentially buying insurance on losing when he makes a side deal, because he'll get a payment if he loses and a bigger payment if he wins. We can buy insurance in case our house burns down, we are robbed, or we get in a car accident. And just like Hellmuth's strategy, it offers peace of mind because there is a smaller cost to loss.

Remind Yourself, "This Is Just One Hand Out of Many"

Hellmuth practices what behavioralists call broad framing: He never feels pressured to play a hand or fold, even if he's down, because he reminds himself it's just one hand out of many. He doesn't just weigh the odds of the single hand he is playing; he considers how it factors into the entire game or tournament.

Since the games Hellmuth plays often last for more than eight hours, it is tempting for him to lose perspective when he's down and take big risks on a single hand to earn his way back. But he then reminds himself to view each hand as part of a larger game.

Think of broad framing as playing the long game. For example, you shouldn't look at your stock portfolio too often. If you are investing for the long term, a bad day on the markets, or even a few bad months, is only a blip. It is not the time to sell your stocks. Framing an individual risky decision as part of a larger gamble will help you think clearly and avoid overreacting to temporary loss.

Avoid Overconfidence to Maintain Focus

Hellmuth is clearly proud of his success. But when it comes to poker, he embraces every opportunity to remain humble. He says it helps him maintain focus. Anything can happen in a game, no matter how skilled you are. When you are up, you can still lose it all.

I spoke to him after a series of big wins. He beat top players in big tournaments and received lots of praise, but one well-known poker player tweeted that Hellmuth was overrated. Rather than defend himself, Hellmuth asked the rival player to list forty players better than him, explaining, "Having this voice doubting me and not giving me any credit—sometimes I use energy from doubters; [it] motivates me."

Hellmuth says overconfidence leads him to take on needless risks and play hands he shouldn't because he is so sure of his skills. It also leads him to lose focus, and maintaining focus is the most critical ingredient for winning poker tournaments or tackling any risk we choose to undertake.

Of course, deciding to become a professional poker player is a risky decision to start with—particularly if it involves dropping out of college. It is the kind of decision that requires lots of optimism. Overconfidence comes naturally to Hellmuth, and he says it can undermine his game.

Most of us don't have the constitution to seek out Twitter criticism on purpose, but Hellmuth's strategy illustrates why we might want to seek out different viewpoints and be open to friendships with people who don't always share our opinions. Avoid group think by forming a team of people who approach problems from different perspectives at work or attempting a civil political discussion with someone who doesn't share your opinion. This strategy can make you more aware of downside risks you need to protect yourself against so that you can see them more clearly.

Hellmuth's example teaches us to be confident enough to take a risk—become a professional poker player or work for a start-up—but once you make the decision, adopt a more risk-averse posture: be less reactive to losing and more consistent in your risk taking by using risk management strategies so you never have too much to lose and can stay focused on success.

Chapter 7

RISK MISPERCEPTION:
I Never Thought I'd Get Caught

*The poet should prefer probable impossibilities
to improbable possibilities.*

—ARISTOTLE

We all fall for it. The Powerball jackpot is the biggest in history, and as you wait in line at a convenience store you see the sign "You can't win if you don't play" and buy a ticket.

Playing does not really increase your odds of winning, at least not in a meaningful way. Mathematically, the difference between zero and one in a kajillion (the odds of winning the lottery jackpot) is too tiny to be considered significant. It does not *feel* that way. Buying the ticket creates the possibility of winning, even if the odds are minuscule, and we put a lot of weight on that tiny possibility.

A sensible, rational risk calculation would not put such a large weight on something so unlikely. If you thought like a financial economist, the weight you'd put on winning the lottery would equal the odds of actually winning. But no one does that, which is why so many people buy tickets. We know the true odds are one in a kajillion, but we behave as if the odds are much more in our favor.

How we interpret probabilities often comes down to how data is presented to us. That sign by the cash register where you buy your ticket—"You can't win if you don't play"—plants the possibility in your head and winning feels more likely. We might not buy a ticket if the sign said "Odds are overwhelming you won't win anyway."

The lottery is just one example of when we assume better odds than we know we actually face. When we make a risky decision, the rational thing to do is to assess risk by weighting each possible outcome by the odds it will actually happen. However, the odds we actually face and the odds we assume when we make a decision often don't match up.

In the case of the lottery, we assume better odds; at other times we underestimate the odds something will happen. Crime is one example of huge risk miscalculation. People commit crimes for many different reasons—out of desperation, bad intentions powered by a thirst for violence, greed, youthful impulsiveness, and lack of legitimate opportunities to earn a living. But all criminals, from an eighteen-year-old small-time drug dealer to a fifty-five-year-old insider trader, share one common characteristic: they don't think they will get caught, even if the odds are they probably will.

If you lived in the New York City area in the 1970s and '80s, odds are you remember Crazy Eddie, an electronics store chain opened by Eddie Antar, his cousin, and his father, for its ubiquitous ad campaign. The ads featured a fast-talking local radio DJ, Dr. Jerry Carroll, shouting about cheap electronics, and ended with "Crazy Eddie, his prices are IN-SA-A-A-A-A-ANE!" The spots became a cultural hallmark, parodied on *Saturday Night Live* and featured in the Tom Hanks movie *Splash*.

It turns out that Crazy Eddie was the front for a large family-run criminal operation. The stores sold cheap electronics, but they made most of their money from underreporting sales, evading income taxes, and pocketing the sales tax. The scheme made the Antars a good amount of money, about $7 million. But they wanted more.

Two years after opening, Eddie gave his fourteen-year-old cousin Sam Antar a job as a stock boy. As Sam told me, "I was the geek of the family, at twelve years old reading the *Wall Street Journal* when everyone else was reading comics. The family saw someone who could be cultivated." Eddie paid for his cousin to go to college and learn accounting, to one day mastermind bigger frauds. "They were paying me to go to college. Picture yourself getting a doctorate in economics and someone is actually paying you to go to school."

When I told him my PhD was paid for, that universities often pay their graduate students, he laughed. "That's good. I was getting a PhD in criminally fucking people."

CRAZY, INDEED

After finishing college in 1979, Sam Antar sat his family down and explained his plan to take Crazy Eddie public; that is, sell their ownership of the electronics chain on the stock market. It would take a few years to prepare for the initial public offering (IPO); the higher the stock price at the IPO, the more money for the Antars. So in the run-up to the IPO, they started to report an increasingly higher fraction of their actual earnings, paying more of the taxes they owed because it would make the stores look more profitable. Growing profits would appeal to investors and drive up the stock price.

Now, risky is running a business that evades taxes. Taking that business public is on another level. It invites greater scrutiny from authorities, and once outsiders owned the company, the Antars would have less control. I asked if the Antars discussed these risks that fateful night in 1979 and Sam explained why they did not:

We'd been a criminal enterprise since 1969, and I'd been part of that criminal enterprise since 1971. In 1979, I had no reason to think that after years of success, I was not going to succeed. Of course I was going to succeed. I am going to take steps and build on prior successes. It gave me the self-confidence to commit crime. Incrementally it gets bigger and bigger. It helped to get to higher and bigger levels.

Sam was working for the auditors, so he knew all the accounting tricks and how to mislead them. The family figured he was smart enough to stay a step ahead of auditors and authorities. And he did for a long time, by distracting these mostly male auditors by staffing the office with young, attractive women.

Still, it is astounding the Antars thought they could operate such a big scam and never get caught. Blasting the airwaves with the most memorable ads of the decade was part of their collective delusion. If you are running a massive fraud, a lower profile would have been a more prudent approach.

In 1984, the stock went public and sold for $8 a share. As profits appeared to rise, so did the size of the chain and the stock price.

At its peak, Crazy Eddie had forty-three stores and reported $353 million in sales, but it was even more profitable on paper thanks to the Antars' manipulation. The family continued to sell their shares of Crazy Eddie, pocketing more than $60 million.

But pressure mounted as business became flat; retail electronics weren't as profitable as they once were. So the Antars upped their criminal risk: they brought their laundered money from the 1970s that was sitting in a foreign bank back into the United States through Panama and used it to inflate revenues. Ironically, they ended up paying all the taxes they had avoided in the past, but it was worth it because they could sell their stock for more money.

Business continued to worsen. In fiscal year 1987, Crazy Eddie reported a profit of $20.6 million when it actually lost millions. Getting rich bound the family together, but as the money started to run out those ties began to fray. Eddie blamed his father for tipping off his wife that he had a mistress. Rumors of family infighting and a slowing electronics market worried investors. The value of Crazy Eddie stock tanked from $21.65 per share to around $5 per share. The remaining Crazy Eddie stock held by the Antars, by now just 5 percent of the company, was nearly worthless. The low price meant Crazy Eddie was susceptible to someone coming in, buying up most of the stock, taking over the business, and uncovering their fraud.

The Antars attempted to buy back most of the company, but they couldn't get financing and were outbid. Another investor beat them to it and promptly ousted the Antars. About two weeks later the new owners discovered Crazy Eddie's inventory was overstated by more than $65 million. The jig was up.

Eddie fled to Israel but was captured there. Sam Antar turned on his family and started working with the FBI and SEC to build their securities fraud case. He got off with fines and six months of house arrest. Eddie was sentenced to eight years in prison, never spoke to Sam Antar again, and "died a bitter man" in 2016.

In addition to Sam Antar, I spent time talking to men who had recently been released from jail at the Fortune Society, a nonprofit in Queens, New York, that helps people coming out of prison reintegrate into society. Most of the men lacked the education and wealth Antar had growing up, but they shared his overconfidence about getting away with their crimes. They lived in communities where many of their friends and relatives went to prison, so I asked if they figured they would get caught one day too. All said some variation of the same thing; as one man put it, "No, I thought I was smarter than all those guys."

Given the nature of their work, risk management is often on most criminals' minds. All the ex-cons I spoke to proudly told me about their hedging strategies. Yet when we think of criminals, we usually don't think of prudent risk takers. This is probably because the decision to commit a crime in the first place is an extremely high-risk choice. Yet people make that choice every day, in large part because the actual probability of getting caught is often much larger than the odds criminals receive.

WE ARE ALL LOUSY AT UNDERSTANDING PROBABILITIES

While you probably haven't decided whether to perpetuate a massive securities fraud, there surely have been times when you've underestimated the odds of a risk not paying off. It could be a big long-odds decision like moving to Hollywood to be a movie star or playing the lottery each week. The odds we put on an event happening—winning an Oscar or the lottery—are how we gauge risk and make decisions. If our gauge is off, and it often is, it can undermine even the most thoughtful risk analysis.

For example, after September 11, 2001, many people were afraid to fly and drove more instead. Statistically, driving is more dangerous; one study estimates the post-9/11 increased fear of flying resulted in 1,600 additional traffic deaths. We all know driving is more dangerous than flying, but the image of a particularly horrific plane crash that is constantly shown on the news changes our risk calculation.

Often the reason we take a big risk comes down to how we perceive probabilities. The most common ways we get probability wrong are:

1. We overestimate certainty. When we do this, it doesn't even occur to us that a decision has any risk associated with it. We assume if we're buying a house, prices will only go up. Or people move to

Hollywood because they believe they are better looking or more talented than most others.

The Antars never thought they'd get caught. They believed Sam would always outsmart the SEC and IRS. The other criminals I interviewed didn't consider getting caught a possibility either.

2. We overestimate the risk of unlikely events. We assume a remote and terrible event is more likely than it is. This is why many people are more afraid of flying than driving, even if they know the odds of dying in a car accident are higher. A plane crash is especially horrific, which is why we put higher odds on its happening.

3. We assume correlations that don't exist. After being dealt a few good hands in poker, you could think you're on a roll and that the next hand is bound to be good too. In fact, each hand you are dealt has nothing to do with the last.

When it comes to crime, getting away with something once, or many times, creates an illusion you'll get away with it the next time. The Antars assumed that because they pulled off tax evasion, they could also get away with securities fraud. Wrong again, and their earlier success led them to take bigger risks to continue the fraud.

4. We put a big weight on very likely or unlikely events and put almost no weight on anything that happens in between. The difference between a 0 percent and 5 percent probability feels huge because it creates possibility. The difference between 100 percent and 95 percent also feels meaningful because it creates or eliminates risk. But the difference between 50 percent and 55 percent barely factors into our decisions. The closer we get to certainty, the more we weight a probability, but mathematically, a 5 percent increase should be given equal weight no matter what.

Sociologists surveyed 1,354 teenagers who were found guilty of a serious offense (almost entirely felony offenses) in the juvenile or adult court systems in Maricopa County, Arizona, and Philadelphia County, Pennsylvania, over a five-year period.

Offenders were asked the odds they thought they'd be arrested for several serious crimes, including fighting, robbery with a gun, stabbing someone, breaking into a store or a home, stealing clothes from a store, vandalism, and auto theft. Over the course of the survey, the sociologists followed up and asked the juveniles what crimes they had committed. If increasing the perceived risk of getting caught was neatly factored into the decision to commit a crime, a 1 percent increase in the odds of being arrested would decrease crime by 1 percent. But humans aren't so simple.

This evidence suggests would-be criminals don't think about risk in a linear way. If the odds of getting caught doubled from 10 percent to 20 percent, people were just as likely to commit a crime. But when the odds increased from 85 percent to 95 percent, that same 10 percent boost deterred many juveniles from reoffending.

We all misperceive probabilities at one time or another. But we aren't doomed to always under- or overestimate risk: how we perceive the odds something will happen depends on how risk is presented to us, and we have more control over that than we realize.

THINKING PROBABILISTICALLY ISN'T NATURAL

The psychologist Paul Slovic has said that defining risk is an exercise in power. Because our brains don't always process probabilities the way economists expect, this leaves room for people to distort our risk perception and alter our behavior. Playing with risk perception can induce all sorts of behaviors, from what we decide to buy, whether we order unhealthy food, whether we commit crime, or what movies we choose to watch.

The lottery slogan "You can't win if you don't play" plants a seed in our heads that winning the lottery is possible, even though it is not even remotely probable. If Google Maps tells us it will take twenty minutes to get to work, that estimate suggests certainty, even though a band of risk really exists around the number Google has not told you about. Netflix might recommend a divisive art house film, suggesting you will surely like it too, because 60 percent of people in your demographic finished watching it. The person selling you a new TV might list all the things that could go wrong, even if they are unlikely, when you are offered an extended warranty. All these subtle forms of communication can alter how we perceive, or are blind to, the risk we actually face.

How we communicate risk can even discourage crime. For many years, people thought the threat of long prison sentences could deter crime. After all, if you face years in prison, the downside risk from crime is more severe: a longer sentence makes crime much riskier. But after decades of long mandatory sentences and plea bargains that resulted in the mass incarceration of millions of Americans, the evidence suggests that long prison sentences did not actually deter much crime. It is not a meaningful, salient risk to someone considering crime. Even knowing people who had gone to prison did not impact the decision of the ex-cons I spoke to because they were convinced they'd get away with it.

The evidence suggests more police on the street is a more effective crime deterrent. We may tell ourselves we'll get away with a crime, but if a police officer is standing on the corner when we're about to hold up a liquor store, it's harder to believe. A stronger police presence makes the risk more real and resonates more; it increases the perception of getting caught to a near certainty, even if the actual punishment remains uncertain. Sam Antar told me he still struggles to stay away from crime. He says following the law was easiest when he worked with the SEC and they watched everything he did.

An important caveat: Not just any kind of policing works; certain tactics are more effective than others. There is less compelling evidence that broken-window policing (arresting people for petty offenses) and "stop and frisk" (detaining civilians who are not committing crimes and searching them for weapons) deter crime in a meaningful way—and these tactics raise questions about the ethics of policing. But studies have found that deploying police in high-crime areas, or hot spots, produces a measurable drop in crime in those (often targeted) places. Community policing (deploying officers who are familiar with the area and the people who live there) can also be effective.

And it is not just these subtle, or not so subtle, messages. Even explicit probabilities can be misleading. In 1995, the UK Committee on Safety of Medicines issued a warning that third-generation birth control doubled the odds of developing a blood clot—a 100 percent increase. Women were terrified: the figure seems to suggest everyone who takes birth control will get a blood clot. Many women stopped taking the pill, which led to an increase in unwanted pregnancies and abortions: there were thirteen thousand additional abortions in England and Wales in 1996.

But the 100 percent figure is misleading. The study actually revealed that one out of seven thousand women developed a blood clot after taking the second-generation pills. This number increased to two out of seven thousand when women took the third-generation pills.

HOW TO TAKE CONTROL

Measuring precise probabilities is a relatively modern invention. Humans have only been able to measure and define risk for a few hundred years. It is not surprising that our brains don't naturally calculate risk assessments that conform to how financial economists and scientists measure probability.

Our ability to make good probability inferences comes down to how risk is presented to us, but better awareness makes us less susceptible to the power of suggestion. The psychologist Gerd Gigerenzer studies how people perceive risk. He argues that people may not understand probabilities, but that does not mean they can't think probabilistically or understand risk. His research shows that frequencies, the actual number of times something happens, resonate better than probabilities because they are more consistent with how humans think and provide the salience we need to make sense of risk.

Let's return to the UK birth control example: a 100 percent increase sounded near certain, but when the information was presented in terms of frequencies—one out of seven thousand and two out of seven thousand—the true risk made more sense. According to Gigerenzer's investigations, when people are shown frequencies instead of probabilities they tend to make sensible, rational decisions and can make sense of probability. His findings also indicate that people are better able to remember frequencies than probabilities.

Gigerenzer believes we should teach risk and probability literacy the same way we teach reading or basic math. Humans aren't born knowing how to read; we teach this skill because it is required to function in the modern world. His research shows people can understand risk, but our brains evolved to understand risk in a certain environment, which is why frequencies resonate with us more than probabilities. Now the environment is changing, and statistical literacy is just as critical to functioning in the modern world as the ability to read.

Thinking probabilistically may not come naturally. But our hidden ability to make sense of risk gives us more power than ever before. Technology has the potential to change how we measure and perceive risk and offers us the ability to make more accurate probability assessments than at any time in the past. Technology companies collect data on everything we do: what movies we watch, what we buy, and where we go. This data can be used to estimate probabilities to help guide our decisions. Soon we will be armed with the most accurate probabilities available. Today's advances may turn out to be as profound as when Fermat and Pascal first measured risk.

But what good are all these estimates of probability if we distort them? Even scarier, our sensitivity to risk perception gives technology companies a new power: the ability to present risk in a way that alters our decision making and plays off our fears. The ability to measure probabilities better can be used to educate us or manipulate us into buying things we don't want or need.

Risk literacy training may not be available in the near future, but we can take it on ourselves now to make sense of the data presented to us. One way to decode the odds facing you is to think in terms of frequencies. It might mean nothing to you to hear that there's a 30 percent chance of rain. Will it rain 30 percent of the day, or is there a 30 percent chance it will rain at some point during the day? Here's another way to think about it: on one hundred days with similar conditions, it rained at some point on thirty of those hundred days. When a friend of a friend wins the lottery, you may think the odds of it happening to you have gone up. Just remember all the people you know, including yourself, who play each week and have never won.

The modern world means we face challenges that require skills we weren't born with. In a data-driven society, we have the ability to estimate the probability that a movie will entertain us, a job will work out, or a crime will land us in jail. Most of us have not been trained in how to understand these probabilities—but that doesn't mean we can't learn to use frequencies to think probabilistically.

GET THE BIGGEST BANG FOR YOUR RISK BUCK

You never get something for nothing. The same usually goes for taking a risk. Risk is the price we pay to get more. And, just like anything else in life, there is no reason to pay more for something than you have to.

When we make a risky decision—to take a different job, to buy a house, to go on a blind date—it is generally true that the potential for a bigger reward comes with more risk. But that doesn't mean more risk always means more reward. Sometimes we face different options that offer the same possible reward, but one comes with more risk than the others. Chapter 8 shows you how to take as little risk as possible while maximizing your reward.

Financial economists consider unnecessary risk inefficient. They argue you can achieve more efficiency through diversification. The result is the same, or greater, reward for less risk—a bargain indeed in risk terms.

Chapter 8

DIVERSIFICATION:
Looking for Efficiency in All the Wrong Places

Put all your eggs in one basket . . . the handle's going
to break. Then all you've got is scrambled eggs.

—NORA ROBERTS, *REMEMBER WHEN*

Facing risk is the cost of getting what we want, and just like any cost, sometimes we can economize and get more for less. We can eliminate unnecessary risk by diversifying, or owning a lot of different assets to avoid putting all of our bets on one asset. Outside of financial economics, this could mean dating multiple people or holding several different jobs in the age of gig work. If you diversify correctly, you get the closest thing that exists to a free lunch. You can get the same, or more, expected reward and face less risk.

In the 1950s and '60s, the idea that you could reduce risk and get the same expected reward was a revelation that changed investment. Now the same idea is catching on and may bring diversity to other fields, even places you would never connect to the stock market, like a stud farm in Kentucky's horse country.

A racehorse is an exceptional creature—a living, breathing investment portfolio. And just like the elusive combination of stocks that promises investors riches each year, a horse with a perfect blend of characteristics is needed to win a major race. A champion horse is just the right size, with a large heart and hips that curve at just the right angle. It needs the right temperament and will to win as well as the right training and jockey to reach its potential. When everything is in place, a racehorse runs so efficiently that it can cover 10 furlongs (about 2,000 meters) in less than two minutes. The same cannot be said about the efficiency of racehorse breeding.

PITY THE TEASER

The breeding shed at Three Chimneys stud farm in Versailles, Kentucky, is not a romantic place. The day I visited, four people wearing black helmets and matching padded vests stood around, humorless and all business. A female horse, or brood mare, was led in from a nearby stable, where a teaser—a less precious horse who minimizes the risk of an unwilling mare injuring the stallion trying to mate with her—had put her in the mood. The teaser is pulled away before he can mount her.*

The mare† stood in the corner of the shed, held steady so she wouldn't kick the stallion that had just entered the stable. This was the legend I'd come to see. His name is Gun Runner, the hottest stallion on the market. He only stopped racing a few months before, so he is still muscular, shiny, and strong. He's the Mick Jagger (in his prime) of horses. A session with him costs $70,000.

I had no idea what to expect during the main event. As it turned out, it wasn't hard to not look squeamish. After some sniffing, Gun Runner

---

* Teasers do get to breed at least once a year with an equally undesirable mare. Breeders provide such opportunities both to be nice and to keep the teaser motivated to do his thankless job.
† Her owner prefers I don't reveal her name.

mounted the mare while one of the helmeted humans held her tail back and another helped Gun Runner penetrate her. About three minutes later, Gun Runner jumped off and things took a clinical turn. One of the humans rushed in to collect his runoff sperm, took it to an adjoining room, and looked at it under a microscope. We all took a peek, and it was good—Gun Runner's sperm runs faster than he does. The helmeted handler put the sperm she collected in a syringe, inserted her arm, elbow deep, into the mare, and deposited it as backup. The handler sighed, took her glove off, and shook my hand.

Gun Runner had to do all this again later that day with a different mare. He was scheduled to breed with 170 mares that season, averaging three a day.

THE STUD MARKET IS INEFFICIENT

Horse people talk about horses the same way the paparazzi discuss celebrities, and Gun Runner is really hot right now. When I tell people I saw him breed, they all nod approvingly. He had a very good racing career and the right pedigree. But what he really has going for him is that he is new to stud, and hype means money. Many serious horse breeders want Gun Runner's sperm . . . at least right now. It's more than likely that his service fee will fall a bit next year when a new stud comes to town. Being new and untested can be valuable.

But Gun Runner is far from the most in demand. Earlier that day at Claiborne Farm I met War Front. His stud fee when I visited in 2018 was $250,000; he earned more than $25 million in 2018 for the syndicate that owns him. In 2016, he earned the same as American Pharoah, the Triple Crown winner that stands at the nearby Coolmore Stud.*

---

* American Pharoah's current stud fee is private information.

War Front has been a stud since 2007 and several of his progeny have very done well—his babies will sell for up to $1.9 million.

Right now, Gun Runner is cashing in on his newness, but nobody really knows if he will ever reach the upper echelons of breeding as War Front has. It takes at least three or four years to know the value of a horse's progeny. In a few years, when Gun Runner's babies start to race, his fee will either skyrocket or crash. This explains why he will breed 170 times in 2018; his owners need to make money while they can. And there is some value, and no cost, to lots of diversification: the more mares he breeds with, the better the odds he'll produce a successful horse. Grant Williamson who, when I visited,* decided which mares Gun Runner would breed with at Three Chimneys Farm, explained the market only rewards the raw number of successful progeny, not the percentage of successful progeny. So if Gun Runner produces three successful horses, his price will soar—even if he fathers two hundred foals that will never race.

Producing a horse that will win races is a crapshoot because, despite the limited gene pool that makes a Thoroughbred a Thoroughbred, no one really knows what lurks in a horse's genes and what traits will be inherited. Traditionally, all the information anyone knows, when deciding a mating plan, is the horse's lineage and how many races the parents and their offspring won, which in turn determines stud fees. But a winning horse does not have a much better chance of producing a good racer. Jill Stowe, an economist at the University of Kentucky who researches the stud market, estimates that in the markets she studied, paying higher stud fees is correlated with *lower* earnings at the racetrack. Something seems to be askew in the stud market.

Horse breeding is like the movie industry, where it's so hard to predict outcomes, there are incentives to reduce risk in the short run at the

---

* He left Three Chimneys after my visit.

expense of worse outcomes in the long run. The system isn't working: breeding is getting more expensive, but the race times of the top horses are not getting faster.

But this might change. Data and science may hold the solution, allowing breeders to make use of a risk reduction strategy straight from financial economics.

HOW BREEDERS REDUCE THEIR RISK

Making a horse is a very risky investment. A brood mare's womb is valuable, and it takes eleven months to produce a foal. Once he or she is born, it takes two to three years of nurturing and training before it is ready to race. From conception to racing, it costs more than $100,000 to make and train a racehorse (not including the stud fee). No one knows if the investment pays off until the horse races. Odds are good it won't race at all. Of the approximately twenty thousand Thoroughbred foals that were born in the United States in 2018, about 30 percent will never start in a race, and only about 8 percent will place in a stakes race and earn significant money at the racetrack. It is a long-term investment with poor odds and little information at every stage.

To manage the risk that the big investment won't pay off, breeders rarely race the horses they make. The horse I saw conceived will probably be sold a year after it is born (at the yearling stage), so the breeder makes some return on his investment before a horse's potential is revealed. Stowe estimates a yearling's sale price is almost entirely explained by parentage.

The yearling may be sold again after a year, when it is two and starting to run short races. At this stage more information is revealed, like how fast it runs in short sprints, but its ability to win big-money races that are run over longer distances is still unclear. It may seem counterintuitive that a fast horse probably won't win the Kentucky Derby, but horses, like people, have different genetic types.

In 2009, scientists sequenced the horse genome, and a few years later the Irish equine geneticist Emmeline Hill discovered the horse "speed gene." Her findings indicated that speed depends on variations found in a horse's myostatin gene (MSTN), which regulates muscle development and muscle fiber type. In horses (and people) this gene determines whether you'll be fast or better suited for long-distance running. In horses, there are three genetic types: sprinters, long-distance runners, and hybrids (horses that have both sprinting and long-distance features and run best when placed at a mile or a little more).

Sprinters tend to sell well when they are young because they are fast and muscular and also appear to be able to run early. But this does not mean they'll be great racehorses; the big-stakes races tend to be a little longer, just over a mile. Horses that have both sprinting and long-distance genes (heterozygotes) are most valuable because they are more versatile and are best suited to middle-distance races like the Kentucky Derby.

Sprinters don't always have the drive or build to persevere in longer races; they often lack what it takes to bring in the very large amounts of money and glory that come from actually winning a big-stakes race. Winning a stakes race really pays off because those horses, like Gun Runner, will eventually earn big stud fees. Yet the market tends to reward sprinters in prerace sales because winning sprints is early observable information. Breeding investors have an opportunity to earn an earlier return on investment and reduce their risk.

Claiborne Farm's bloodstock manager (the person who decides which horses mate at stud farms), Bernie Sams, is a longtime horse breeder. He is a large man, with a shock of gray hair—exactly what you'd expect if you imagined what a bloodstock manager looks like. He selects which mares from Claiborne or another farm will breed with War Front. Sams will get more requests than War Front can possibly manage. He picks mares that will maximize the odds of producing successful progeny, which keeps up the stud fee.

In his slow, deliberate way of speaking, Sams explained that horses that do well at yearling sales need to look pretty and have a famous father: "Everyone wants a horse that sells well, is fast, and will win the Kentucky Derby. But you can't get all three at once."

INBREEDING

Horse breeders have a short-term economic incentive to inbreed their horses. Decades ago, a desirable stallion bred with sixty or seventy mares a year, but now the hottest ones will breed with nearly two hundred. So Thoroughbreds have become increasingly inbred, even though this inbreeding is inefficient: breeders spend a small fortune on stud fees and face long odds of producing a horse that can race, let alone win.

Thoroughbred horses are inbred by definition: 95 percent of modern Thoroughbreds are thought to trace their ancestry to a single horse, the Darley Arabian, born in 1700. Dr. Mathew Binns, an equine geneticist and a partner at Equine Analysis Systems, a consulting service that assesses horses for investment and breeding using science, estimates that inbreeding has increased among Thoroughbred horses in the last forty years. The increase started to become noticeable in the 1990s, a few years after 1986 tax reform increased incentives to breed commercially (selling a horse before it races), a practice that eventually became the industry norm.* Despite the increase in inbreeding,† Binns says it's

---

* Until the 1960s, when commercial breeding became more profitable, breeders generally did breed to race, and getting a good horse was the goal. According to Frank Mitchell, a journalist and the director of biomechanics at DataTrack International, commercial breeding really took off in the 1980s, when tax reform made passive income less profitable and decreased the incentives to take a long-term risk on a horse. Since then, most breeders sell their horses long before they ever race, when parentage is the only reliable information.

† Inbreeding was further accelerated by better veterinary practice that allowed one stallion to serve many more mares than it had in the past; as a result, fewer stallions retire each year, continuing to serve more mares, thus making the gene pool even shallower.

important to have some perspective: "The average Thoroughbred is still less inbred than a pure-bred dog."

Possibly the most prolific modern racehorse was Northern Dancer, who was a Kentucky Derby and Preakness winner. Northern Dancer's stud career lasted more than twenty years and spanned multiple continents, producing many progeny who also had exceptional racing careers. At its peak in 1984, his stud fee was $500,000, more than $1.2 million in 2018 dollars, six years before his death in 1990.

But he lives on. Today, almost every single Thoroughbred is related to Northern Dancer, often on both their mother's and father's sides, multiple times. According to David Dink, a Kentucky-based writer who has spent his career studying Thoroughbred bloodlines, Northern Dancer was present in the bloodlines of 96.5 percent of the 38,821 foals sold between 2012 and 2015. Dink says Northern Dancer was present two to three times in the lineage of 64 percent of the horses. He was present four times or more in 20 percent of the foals.

The economics of breeding has created incentives to sire more Hapsburgs* (albeit beautiful ones) for two reasons. First, a yearling's father largely determines its value, and there is a fairly small pool of desirable stallions that will bring in big money at yearling auctions. There are only so many champions new to stud and even fewer racehorses with successful offspring.

Second, inbreeding increases the odds of getting a sprinter, a horse that also sells well. Sprinters are homozygotes: if you breed two sprinters, you get a sprinter. Northern Dancer's gene type is unknown, but Emmeline Hill suspects he was a heterozygote (with sprinter and distance genes, as he won longer races). She says there's a "high likelihood" he had at least one sprinting gene, which, when mixed with a hybrid mare, will produce a sprinter 25 percent of the time. If the mare is a sprinter (she has two sprint genes), there's a 50 percent chance the foal

---

* Austrian monarchs notorious for family inbreeding that resulted in large facial features, disease, and infertility.

will be a sprinter too. If both horses are sprinters, breeders are guaranteed a sprinter offspring. Thus, if you keep breeding horses with sprinting genes—generation after generation—you increase the number of sprinters and the odds that the next generation will be full of sprinters too. A 2012 article in *Nature Communications* estimates a significant increase in sprinters through more selective breeding, which can be traced back to Northern Dancer's sprint gene.

Most horse inbreeding occurs between third and fourth cousins, and the horses are rebred many times. Inbreeding among cousins once or twice may be harmless or even beneficial, but if you keep inbreeding, negative effects could emerge. After a while, inbreeding becomes high risk, high reward. It doubles down on a horse's characteristics, which can be good or bad. Inbred horses tend to be fast sprinters, but they are also more likely to be barren. Binns has noticed a slight increase in barren mares with increased inbreeding. He explained to me that the bones of inbred horses may be less dense, making them more prone to injury.

After the market changed, so did horses. Better technology and training techniques produced increasingly fast horses from the 1930s through the 1980s, but in the 1980s, times for the big races plateaued and stayed flat until recently.* Ed DeRosa, director of marketing for Brisnet, a subsidiary of Churchill Downs, says their data shows that horses may have gotten even slower in the last ten to fifteen years.

Several developments could explain slower horses. As horses have become more expensive in the sales ring, the industry has become more focused on safety: tracks for long races are sandier and drier to provide more cushion and make horses run slower. (DeRosa claims his data controls for changes in track conditions.) Horse are given fewer

---

* These researchers studied British horse race times from 1850 to 2012. Two-year-old horses that ran sprint races started to get faster in 1997. But race times for older horses that run longer, high-profile races like the Derby have not improved. This study was limited to British horses.

hormones and steroids* than they were in the 1980s and '90s. Drug-free horses cannot be trained as hard. Generations of inbreeding may also be taking their toll. The biologist Mark Denny speculates that more inbreeding may mean less genetic innovation, which is how species normally evolve and produce faster animals.

THE BENEFITS OF DIVERSIFICATION

If the goal were instead to produce a horse that wins races, the risk reduction strategy would be different. Breeders would get a higher return for their stud fee if they diversified the Thoroughbred gene pool by breeding their mares with one of many stallions, not just the select few. There is little evidence that mating with a race winner significantly increases the odds of winning at the racetrack. Another horse might produce similar, or better, results for less money. It may even bring some diversity back to the gene pool and increase the odds of producing a hybrid (heterozygote) horse.

In finance, people eliminate needless risk by diversifying too, by owning more than one stock. Suppose it is January 1993 and you have $25,000 to invest for the next twenty years. You are interested in the burgeoning tech sector and are torn between buying Apple or Hewlett-Packard stock. Both companies look like they have a promising future, and their stocks have performed similarly in the past, with an average return of about 11 percent a year. At that point, investing in either seemed to offer similar prospects and risk; they were both established companies in the tech sector and growing.

If you put all your money in Apple stock, in twenty years you'd have more than $1 million. If you bought Hewlett-Packard with that same $25,000, you'd have only $57,000. Fifty-seven thousand dollars may not

---

* Steroids have been outlawed except under certain circumstances for more than five years and are banned completely in international competition.

sound so bad, but if you bought a lower-risk five-year bond fund in 1993 you'd have almost $77,000 by 2013 and wouldn't have had to deal with the stress of the stock price jumping up and down with ill-fated mergers.

In hindsight, Apple was a much better bet. The problem was that in 1993 it was impossible to know that. Apple's prospects looked worse: Steve Jobs was four years away from his return to the company, and the iPhone was not even a twinkle in his eye. Apple's stock went down more than 75 percent after 1993, before it took off.

At the time, your best bet would have been to invest half your money in Apple and the other half in Hewlett-Packard. If you did, twenty years later you'd have $604,000—much less than if you had just invested in Apple, but considering what you knew in 1993, it would have reduced risk and offered a similar expected return.

You can reduce risk even more by buying stocks in a completely un-related industry. A meltdown in technology will not impact the auto in-dustry as much, so owning General Motors will mean less risk to your portfolio if there is another technology stock crash.

In chapter 5, we explored the two main kinds of risk, idiosyncratic and systematic. If you diversify enough and buy hundreds or thou-sands of stocks, you can eliminate all idiosyncratic risk specific to one stock—you'd never even notice what happens to Apple or Hewlett-Packard.

Diversification is a powerful risk reduction tool. In an uncertain economy, gig work, or a "side hustle," is a form of diversification to help reduce your idiosyncratic job risk. If your regular job cuts your hours or lays you off, a side hustle, like driving for Uber or Lyft, or small consult-ing jobs, can be your fallback.

You can diversify to eliminate idiosyncratic risk, but you're still ex-posed to systematic or market risk—the odds the whole stock market will crash or there's a recession that lowers the demand not just for your full-time job but also for your side hustle.

A SELF-DESCRIBED NERD STARTS A REVOLUTION

Finding the best combination of assets that deliver high reward and low risk is the holy grail for portfolio managers, just as finding the two horses that will produce the next Secretariat is for bloodstock managers. Both traditionally relied on guesswork and intuition and got mediocre results. But then, in finance, a data revolution and better mathematical techniques transformed portfolio management, and finding the ultimate portfolio became more scientific and less risky.

In 1952, an economics doctoral student named Harry Markowitz started research on the stock market at the University of Chicago. A native Chicagoan, Markowitz had been a quiet, studious child who liked math, played the violin, and avoided sports.

In the 1950s, few economists took much interest in the stock market, which still had a bad reputation more than twenty years after the Great Depression. When Markowitz started his PhD, only one in sixteen adults owned stock—now nearly half do—and investment management was largely more art than science. It consisted of picking a few dozen stocks that offered the highest possible return for wealthy people, and little thought was given to explicitly reducing risk. For most academics, the stock market did not seem interesting or worthy of research.

At the time, economists assumed that a stock's value was based entirely on a company's expected future profits, which struck Markowitz as an odd assumption. If future profit levels were the only predictor of value, then everyone would only pick one or two stocks, the ones with the highest expected return. Why would anyone bother owning dozens of stocks, like most investors did? Markowitz was struck with the notion that people should be interested in risk as well as return.

Markowitz's realization provided the intellectual foundation for modern finance to emerge as a discipline within economics—the study of risk and how to manage it. He discovered that when we focus only on returns, we often end up taking unnecessary risk because we try to pick only winners (which is impossible). If we picked stocks that balanced each other out instead, risk would be reduced and, on average, we'd get the same, or a better, return.

In all areas of economics, economists presume we live in a world with scarce resources. The world has only so much oil, gold, and iron ore. A central question in economics is how we can use these resources in the best way, or how to minimize waste.

Markowitz applied the same idea to financial markets. In finance, risk is the input and reward is the output. And just as there's an efficient way to use a limited amount of iron to make as many cars as possible, there's an efficient way to select stocks. Markowitz argued that diversification—owning lots of stocks that have different risk characteristics that can offset each other—was how investors could create efficient portfolios.

Markowitz set off a revolution in financial thinking, shifting the focus from returns to risk. His ideas really took off in the 1960s when financial data and computing power became more available. Mutual funds, portfolios of different assets marketed to investors, had existed since the eighteenth century, but the market was small* and stock selection was based on human judgment, not science. Access to data and computing made it possible for academics and investors to measure how stock prices moved in the past, how much one went up when another went down. The data and new mathematical techniques made it possible to find more efficient stock portfolios that got bigger rewards for less risk. Instead of holding just ten or fifteen stocks, the modern mutual fund, a collection of hundreds or thousand of stocks, became more popular. Some stocks can reduce portfolio risk more than others, but as long as a stock's price does not behave in the exact

---

* With the notable exception of investment trusts in the 1920s, but their popularity waned after the stock market crash.

same way as the rest of the portfolio, adding more stocks reduces idiosyncratic risk.

About a decade after Markowitz first published his paper on portfolio selection, John Andrew "Mac" McQuown, the director of management sciences at Wells Fargo, was introduced to Markowitz's ideas through friends at the University of Chicago and came up with the idea of an index fund—another revolution in finance. An index fund is a portfolio of many stocks, hundreds or thousands. How much you own of each stock is based on a set rule, like how big a company is. If the value of General Electric's stock makes up 2 percent of the entire stock market, 2 percent of your portfolio is in General Electric. McQuown started the first index funds and sold them to big investors like pension funds in 1971. A few years later John Bogle started Vanguard and sold index funds to everyday investors.

Because there is no special sauce in index funds and no special genius who knows which stocks will pay off big, they charge lower fees. The creation of the index fund meant everyday investors could easily invest in lots of stocks, thousands of stocks all over the world, and get the benefits of diversification for low cost and almost no effort.

Investment firms were skeptical of index funds—after all, they make their money by promising they know the right stocks to buy, even though there is little evidence to prove that claim. Study after study shows that actively managed mutual funds, the ones that contain professionally picked stocks, don't offer higher returns than index funds after adjusting for risk and fees.

Still, the idea that people could pick the next Apple remains tempting. Diversification may offer the same expected gain for less risk, but you still give up the ginormous returns from picking the next Amazon or Google. Take the quote, widely attributed to superstar investor Warren Buffett, found on dozens of financial websites that offer tips on how to beat the market: "Diversification is protection against ignorance. It makes little sense if you know what you are doing."

If you had invested $25,000 in Apple in 1993, you would have had $1 million twenty years later; the same $25,000 investment in the S&P 500 (the five hundred most valuable stocks in the United States) would have been worth just $80,000 by 2013. It's easy to think that you would have picked Apple back in the day, and if you actually did, that you'll be able to pick the next big one, but it's much harder to consistently pick winners—that's why Warren Buffett is a crazy-rich superstar.

Diversification can also reduce risk in a technology-powered economy, even outside finance—in our jobs, in our friendships, in our love lives. Having more friends increases the odds someone will be available when you need them. Dating more people helps you figure out what you need in a relationship and prevents you from overinvesting in someone before you know them. Of course, you give up the extreme upside here too: relationships are slower to form, or we may become overwhelmed with unlimited options. But until we find the people we want to take a chance on, diversification helps mitigate the risk that we make a bad choice.

HORSE BREEDING'S ANSWER TO HARRY MARKOWITZ?

Enhanced technology produces better data that often results in more diversification and less risk. It sparked a revolution in finance that made index and mutual funds how most households invest in the stock market. And now different ride- and task-sharing apps use data and algorithms so we can pick up gig work to diversify our income. The same technology is even diversifying our love lives (think Tinder). Horse breeding could be next.

Horse breeding would benefit from more diversification. Inbreeding is expensive for such a high risk/high reward outcome, but data and technology might incentivize breeders to bring together horses with complementary features instead of betting on a handful of potential big winners. This would bring more diversity to breeding, just as mutual funds did in financial markets.

The incentives are different depending on whether you plan to sell or race a horse. If breeders raced their own horses instead of selling them, they might pair two different mares and stallions to breed. "Selling well" takes having the right pedigree and the characteristics of a sprinter, both of which encourage inbreeding. But maximizing the odds of producing "a good horse" is more complicated.

Ideally, breeders would match the male and female characteristics, balancing out weaknesses—bad hips are paired with good ones, strong knees with weak ones, and so on, doubling down on strengths. According to Dr. David Lambert, a veterinarian and the president of Equine Analysis Systems, a race winner like Gun Runner is a bit of a genetic freak. Most of those unusual qualities are hard to reproduce and, if they don't all line up just so, they will produce a slow horse.

For example, winners often have large hearts. A normal horse heart weighs only eight or nine pounds; Secretariat's was twenty-one pounds. That extra cardiovascular potential is critical, but it doesn't translate into running fast unless it meshes with a horse's other features. Lambert says it's like putting a Ferrari engine in a Subaru. It is better to mate an extraordinary horse with an ordinary horse, he argues, or pair two horses with slightly above-average features. This runs counter to the conventional wisdom to mate two of the highest-performing horses available, which can produce foals with lots of freakish features that don't always work well together.

Inbreeding is a lot like just investing in the one stock you think will be the next Apple. There's a chance lightning will strike, and the payoffs will be huge. But it's a lot more likely that you'll end up with a lame portfolio. Diversification increases the odds of producing a good horse that will make money at the races, for a lower stud fee.

But this is not how breeding is done—for now.

Geneticists and data scientists are hoping to change the industry by providing more information on the horses, like their speed genes or heart size, just as data and computing changed portfolio management. It means buyers will have a better sense of a horse's racing potential at yearling auctions, which may drive sales based on horse quality rather than who the sire is. Information has the potential to align the incentives of breeders and owners, and breeding "a good horse" will be the same thing as a "horse that can sell."

And data can also be useful to create a "good horse" by identifying the best match for a mare. Breeders, just like portfolio managers, would aim to balance out different characteristics to reduce the risk that a horse can't race. If the goal was producing the best runner, there's less incentive to pay $100,000 for a stallion's sperm just because he won races and his progeny are sprinters. Instead, stud fees would be driven by matching the exact right characteristics, increasing diversity and the probability of getting a great racer. A bigger population of horses will be able to breed; a larger pool of sires would also reduce stud fees and produce more "good horses"—the best of both worlds.

Byron Rogers, a data scientist and bloodstock agent at Performance Genetics, explained how smarter breeding choices reduce risk by lowering the number of unraceable horses. Emmeline Hill says genetics has the potential to narrow the distribution of outcomes when it comes to breeding. It can't guarantee you'll make a Kentucky Derby winner, but it will increase the number of horses you'll produce that will have respectable racing careers, for a smaller stud fee.*

The science remains controversial. No one believes you can ever perfectly genetically engineer a horse to win big races, since the way genetic traits play out is unpredictable. Using science to make a Kentucky Derby winner is even more elusive than picking a portfolio of future Apple stocks. Nonetheless, more genetic diversification has the potential to

---

* Even if it is an inefficient market, investing in racehorses is still very risky; it is best to stick to index funds.

change the economics of horse breeding. Who knows? It could even mean a new world record at the Kentucky Derby.

Horse breeding will always be risky, even riskier than investing in the stock market. Using data to achieve optimal genetic diversification can reduce the idiosyncratic risk of perpetuating freakish genetic features or spending a fortune to produce a horse that will never race. But there still remains systematic risk because the industry is so dependent on a few wealthy investors. Just as diversification can't reduce the risk the whole stock market will crash, it can't make the breeding industry less sensitive to a bad economy where horse speculators have less money to gamble. Managing systematic risk requires other kinds of risk management, explained in the next two chapters.

BE THE MASTER OF YOUR DOMAIN

We face risk every time we make a decision about the future and subject ourselves to what might happen, for good or bad. But our decision process doesn't end there; we have some control over how a risk plays out.

Risk management is how we can stack the odds in our favor. In chapter 4, risk was represented by a picture of the things we can imagine happening and how probable they are, or a probability distribution. The pictures represented risk profiles for different kinds of movies. In each picture the x-axis, or the domain, represented all the potential profit scenarios. The wider the distribution, the more risk. Risk management takes charge of your domain, so you can alter the shape that picture takes.

We can do this in two different ways. Chapter 9 describes the first way: hedging. When we hedge, we give up some of our potential gains in exchange for reducing the chance of loss; in statistical terms, it cuts off the upper and lower tails of risk.

The second method, explained in chapter 10, is insurance. With insurance, we pay someone else a fixed amount to take on our downside and we still keep the upside. With hedging you give up some upside in exchange for getting rid of downside. With insurance you get rid of downside risk, but the upside, or upper tail, is still all yours (minus the cost of insurance). Of course, the opportunity for no downside and the potential for unlimited upside sometimes comes at a steep cost.

Each of these risk reduction methods can be flipped around: instead of being used to reduce risk, they can be used to increase it, and with it, our potential reward. This is always tempting, especially if we think we're insured. Chapter 11 discusses how to find the right balance.

Chapter 9

DE-RISKING:
The Art of the Hedge

It is only by being bold that you get anywhere. If you
are a risk-taker, then the art is to protect the downside.

—RICHARD BRANSON

Think of the last story you heard about a successful business-person who took a huge risk and despite no way to manage it charged ahead anyway. After some tensions and near misses, the risk works out and the fearless leader becomes incredibly rich. But whether we revel in this person's abilities or, because the gamble failed, never hear his or her name usually comes down to luck or timing.

A story we can actually learn from is the story of a businessperson who knew how to hedge risk. Hedging involves taking less risk by giving up big gains to avoid big losses. What takes skill is knowing exactly how to find the right balance between risk and reward, or knowing exactly how much risk to take. And when someone is born into poverty, hedging risk, rather than just shooting for the moon, is what it really takes to beat the odds.

A rnold Donald, the CEO of Carnival, the world's largest cruise company, has one such story. In his office in Doral, Florida, he sits across from me behind a huge, grand desk, the walls papered with pictures of him and various world leaders. He is a distinguished, regal man in his sixties, but his eyes light up like an eight-year-old boy's when he starts to talk about games. "I played Monopoly a lot. The board game. Honestly I've never lost," he says proudly. "I'm vicious, you know. I haven't played in forever now. [My brother] was, like, eight years older than me and I'd still whoop him."

Donald has spent most of his life winning by overcoming long odds in a world that seemed stacked against him. He's one of a handful of black American CEOs of large companies and grew up "dirt poor" in the Ninth Ward of New Orleans under segregation. But neither poverty nor racism have ever stopped Donald. He says the secret is to maximize the probability of getting what you want, and he perfected this strategy growing up as the youngest in a family of five.

Donald learned the perils of taking on leverage and too much risk early. He'd borrow money from his father, buy candy in bulk, resell it to his sisters at a steep markup, then pay back his father and keep the profits. This strategy worked until his sisters found his stash and took his supply. It was an important lesson for young Donald. Even now, he generally does not take risks when he can lose big.

By junior high, he was identified as exceptional. He went to St. Augustine High School, an all-black, all-male Catholic school in New Orleans, where students received a great education and were instilled with high expectations. Three times a day the PA system would boom out the same message: "Gentlemen, prepare yourselves because one day you're going to run the world."

Donald got the message that anything was possible. The best colleges wanted him—and many of his classmates—badly and recruited him.

Young Donald saw a world without limits, but making the highest-risk choice wasn't part of his strategy to succeed. He often tempers his ambitions and is willing to take slightly less to maximize the probability that things will work out. Consider his childhood ambition: he dreamed of being a businessman, specifically, to be "the general manager at a Fortune 50 science-based, global company."

With the world at his feet, it sounds like a relatively modest ambition. Most high school students dream of being a professional athlete, a successful entrepreneur, or a CEO. But in the 1960s, landing a stable job at a big firm and rising through the ranks was the most likely path to success. It was also a world away from the Ninth Ward. Donald may have sensed unlimited opportunity, but taking a big risk and failing was not an option for him:

> I'm not sure I was risk averse. What I would say is I was statistically oriented. My philosophy in life . . . I don't know where I picked this up. Some of it came from playing Monopoly. But my philosophy in life was maximize the probability of success. And whenever I thought something out, I said, How can I rig this so that I have a greater probability of success?

When it came to college, he hedged again. After a visit to Carleton College, Donald realized he wanted to attend a small liberal arts school. His enthusiasm for Carleton was probably enhanced by meeting his future wife during his campus visit. Donald knew he needed to study economics and engineering, two separate degrees, to maximize the probability of meeting his career goal. Carleton did not offer this option.

So he made a deal with Stanford University, which had also offered him a full scholarship. Stanford would keep his scholarship waiting for him while he studied economics at Carleton for three years. After that, he'd transfer to Stanford and complete a two-year engineering degree. It was a way to get the best of both worlds: the liberal arts experience he wanted and the Stanford engineering degree.

During his sophomore year at Carleton, Donald married his college sweetheart, who also received a place at Stanford's engineering school but no scholarship. Rather than take on the financial risk of student loans, they went to Washington University in St. Louis, where they both had scholarships.

After he graduated, he took a job at Monsanto, the now-notorious agricultural technology company based in St. Louis. Donald, a self-described outspoken "hothead" in his youth, did all he could to succeed in the corporate world. On the advice of one of his colleagues, Donald shed his Louisiana accent and his sideburns to fully embrace the life of a midwestern corporate executive.

Donald quickly climbed the corporate ladder, making general manager by age thirty-two and continuing his rise through the ranks by taking an interest in the science of agriculture as well as the business. Philip Needleman, a former colleague of Donald's who was head of research and development at Monsanto, said this was a rare combination at the time. "He was the only African-American senior person I was aware of at Monsanto. His performance was hard nosed, measured by quarterly business and where sales were at."

Donald held several leadership roles before becoming president of Monsanto's Consumer and Nutrition Sector. Then in 2000, after a twenty-three-year career at Monsanto, he took an uncharacteristic unhedged risk and struck out on his own, away from the safety of the corporate hierarchy he'd grown up in. With a group of investors, he spun off Monsanto's artificial sweetener business, or "low-calorie high-intensity sweeteners" as he calls them, into a new company named Merisant; Donald became the CEO. But the artificial sweetener business is fickle. Merisant struggled when the market turned from their product, Equal, to another alternative, Splenda. Donald stepped down as CEO after three years, took a good severance package, and stayed on as chairman until 2005. Merisant filed for bankruptcy in 2009.

After he left Merisant, Donald had made enough money that he decided to cash out and retire at the young age of fifty-one, having achieved his goals. He spent his time serving on various corporate boards and taking small risks, cruising through life.

Retirement lasted eight years before he got the call from Carnival Corporation. Carnival was a family-operated business; Micky Arison, the CEO at the time, was the son of the founder. When they approached Donald, Carnival had just faced a series of high-profile setbacks. In 2012, the *Costa Concordia* (a Carnival-owned ship) wrecked off the coast of Italy; thirty-two passengers and crew members died and the captain abandoned the ship.

A year later, the *Carnival Triumph*'s engine caught fire and the ship lost power while out to sea. The outage compromised sanitation for the four long days it took to tow the ship to port; the media dubbed the ill-fated voyage "the poop cruise." CNN showed the slow tow in real time and broadcast horror stories of travelers confronting raw sewage.

These would be massive setbacks for any company, but they were particularly severe blows to the cruise industry's image. When you book a cruise, you give up the promise of a unique adventure and solitude in exchange for a risk-free vacation. Sure, it can feel less exciting and personal than trekking through the Andes or camping on the beach in Bali, but a cruise vacation is almost certain to go well, or at least smoothly. With cruising, hotels are never overbooked, the food is predictable and plentiful, rental cars don't break down, and activities are all prearranged.

But if things go wrong, they go really wrong. The tail risk is being stranded on a sewage-laden ship in the middle of an ocean or worse. If the tail risk no longer seems improbable, the most appealing part of cruising loses its luster.

Donald may not have seemed like a natural fit. He had been on the

Carnival board for more than a dozen years, but his career as an agricultural executive did not appear to lend itself to cruising. His colleagues from Monsanto were surprised when they heard that Donald had joined Carnival: "He's a very ambitious fellow, but what does he know about running cruise liners?"

The job seemed like the biggest risk Donald had ever taken. But his career/life strategy—maximizing the odds of getting what you want by finding the right balance of risk and reward—was exactly what the cruise industry needed. As he said to me, "You know there's risk, so you try to maximize the probability of success. And it's not like you don't feel there's any risk. You believe you can address the risks. And that's the difference."

Anticipating the risks of what can go wrong is a skill Donald has developed over the years. But merely anticipating the risks is not enough; he also takes steps to make sure that if something does go wrong it inflicts as little damage as possible. Sometimes he insures the risks he foresees, and most often he hedges by taking less risk to begin with.

HEDGING

We use the word "hedge" anytime we reduce risk; for example, when we "hedge our bets," when we keep our options open. In finance, hedging has a more precise meaning: de-risking, or taking less risk. It involves giving up your potential gains if things go well, in exchange for reducing the odds of things going wrong. Overall, de-risking increases the odds of your getting what you want, but you must give up the possibility of getting more.

Suppose two things in life make you happy: money and your local football team. If your team is playing in a big game, a hedge would be betting $100 against your team with 3–1 odds they'll lose. If your team loses you feel that sting of loss, but at least you get $300, which is some consolation. If your team wins, you experience the thrill of victory, but that victory is a little less sweet because you are out $100.

Hedging is one of the oldest and simplest financial strategies, but it is often neglected or confused with diversification. Diversification eliminates unnecessary risk by owning shares in lots of different assets; it could be pooling risk with other celebrity photographers or owning an index fund that contains lots of stocks in your investment portfolio. Your expected return is the same, but risk is reduced, because no matter what happens, odds are something you own will pay off. Diversification can eliminate idiosyncratic risk, but it does not help you with systematic risk like the entire stock market crashing the day before you are set to retire. Diversification helps you construct the best risky option, but you still have to manage the remaining risk.

Hedging is determining how much of that risky option you want to or have to take to achieve your goal. And, unlike diversification, it comes at a cost. You must give up some of your expected gains, because you are taking less risk at the cost of less reward.

Hedging is more precise because it takes more planning and a clear goal. It requires thinking through your goal, whether it's more wealth, a career as a high-powered executive, or feeling good about your football team, and then doing something that reduces the risk that the goal won't be reached. Hedging does not differentiate between systematic and idiosyncratic risk, but it can reduce both types.

Remember Santiago Baez, the paparazzo from chapter 5? He faced lots of systematic and idiosyncratic risk in the celebrity photo business, since the industry was changing and the odds of catching a celebrity at the right time was always low. Baez loved the work, and on a good day would make big money. He reduced his idiosyncratic risk by forming an alliance with other photographers. But a lot of risk remained because the market was so unstable. He faced more systematic risk, more days when he earned little and fewer days when he got a major payday. This forced him to quit. Instead, if he had wanted to hedge, he could have taken a few days off from the streets and taken a job photographing a wedding. He'd have given up the excitement and potential returns of catching that big celebrity photo at the right time, but he would have gotten certain income no matter what happened in the celebrity world. It would also have been a more stable income source; the celebrity photograph market might change, but people always want wedding pictures.

Or suppose you decide to become a social media influencer. You figure you can make money and fill the hole in your soul if you get lots of followers, likes, and retweets on Twitter. The more active you are, the more likely you'll tweet that perfect pithy comment, leading to a celebrity retweeting you, and fame and fortune (or just a brief rush of satisfaction). But tweeting constantly increases the risk of saying something wrong or even offensive, which could negatively impact your career. You can hedge this risk by tweeting only several times a day and only tweeting things you've thought about carefully. You miss out on the upside of Internet fame, but you reduce the risk of becoming a social pariah.

INVEST MORE IN A RISK-FREE ASSET

The simplest way to hedge is to simply take less risk. Suppose your goal is to have $12,000 in five years to pay for your son's first year of college, and you have $12,000 today. You're hoping to make his first year of college extra special and spend another $3,000 so he can live in a nicer dorm. Your financial adviser tells you a well-diversified stock portfolio is expected to earn 8 percent a year. That means on average you can expect about $17,600 in five years, the money you need for tuition and a nice dorm room plus an extra bonus. But the stock market is risky. There is no promise it will actually return 8 percent a year and there's a chance could lose money. Say the stock market drops 40 percent after the first year. Even if the market earns 8 percent each of the next four years, by year five you'll only have about $9,800.

To protect against this risk your adviser suggests a hedging strategy: invest $6,000 of your money in bonds. They only offer a 3 percent return, but you will definitely earn 3 percent each year. Your expected return will be 5.5 percent a year, lower than 8 percent, but odds are you will have about $15,000 in five years. If the stock market drops in the first year and then recovers, you'll end up with about $12,000 in five years. Hedging by buying bonds relieves some of the risk of losing money, in exchange for giving up the possibility of that extra $2,600.

Many personal finance columns will tell you to invest your retirement account in a mutual fund, a collection of stocks, instead of a single stock. That is good advice, but it is not a complete retirement investment strategy since these funds only offer diversification. A more complete strategy hedges the remaining risk. Hedging for retirement requires figuring out your goal: stable income, a big pile of money, or some combination of the two. You can hedge the risk that stocks won't pay off by investing some of your retirement account in a mutual fund and the rest in an appropriate risk-free asset like short- or long-term bonds.

The effect is simply taking less risk, giving up some potential good returns in exchange for reducing the risk of loss. This strategy can be used outside of finance. It is how Donald often approaches risk; he formulates a goal and maximizes the odds of realizing it by taking just enough risk to make it happen. He is willing to give up extra upside if it means he's protected in the worst-case scenario. He used this strategy when he chose his college major and career, and he uses it to manage Carnival.

Hedging is a common business strategy. Airlines often hedge the risk that oil prices will go up by entering into contracts where no matter what happens to oil prices in the future they will pay a certain price for fuel.* Oil prices might fall and the airline still must pay the higher price they agreed to. But if oil prices go up, the airline pays less than the market rate. The certainty allows airlines to make long-term decisions and plan. They give up the chance of extra profits from cheap oil in exchange for eliminating the risk of oil prices going up.

Modern Finance

Another expert in hedging risk was David Bowie, who in addition to being a brilliant musician was also an extremely gifted risk tactician.

A musician usually signs with a record label early in his or her career. The label offers the artist a large payment (that is, large for a young, struggling musician who is poor and very excited to be discovered) and in exchange the label owns a large share of the royalties the artist's work generates.

This is a terrible deal if a musician becomes successful. Coupled with bad money management, it is why many famous musicians plead poverty or declare bankruptcy, but it can actually be a fair risk exchange. If the artist's career never takes off, he or she still gets the money and the label gets the royalties, which aren't worth much. Most musicians won't be successful, and will never earn more than their advance.

As a teenager David Bowie was shrewd and confident; both he and his manager believed he'd be one of the few who'd make it big. When he made his deal, he insisted on retaining future ownership of his music and took a smaller advance as part of the deal. The people who signed him thought they were getting a great bargain. Odds were good the skinny teenager's music wouldn't be worth much in the future anyhow. Bowie took a risk on himself and it paid off.

---

* The counterparty is taking on the oil-price risk.

About thirty years later, Bowie faced a different problem. He was in his fifties, and the future of music looked uncertain. Napster had recently started file sharing, so now music could be shared and heard without anyone paying for it. It was no longer clear how much music royalties would be worth going forward. Bowie considered taking the opposite bet he did years before, and selling his royalties. He said in 2002:

> The absolute transformation of everything that we ever thought about music will take place within 10 years, and nothing is going to be able to stop it. I see absolutely no point in pretending that it's not going to happen. I'm fully confident that copyright, for instance, will no longer exist in 10 years, and authorship and intellectual property is in for such a bashing.

Yet Bowie was still reluctant to sell his songs, which he considered his "babies." Meanwhile, his business manager was working with David Pullman, a fast-talking, Wharton-educated banker, who had a better idea. He never saw an asset he couldn't de-risk.

Pullman entered finance in the early days of mortgage-backed securities. Mortgage-backed securities got a bad name during the 2008 financial crisis because the technology was used to take ill-advised, risky bets on people who bought houses they couldn't afford. But the basic idea is fairly simple and smart. When a bank sells a mortgage, it is owed a stream of income over many years—the mortgage payments. This money is illiquid; that is, it can't be accessed until each payment is due. If the bank wants the money sooner or wants to get rid of the risk that the mortgage won't be repaid, it can sell the mortgage as a bond. An investor pays a big chunk of money to the bank, and in exchange the investor gets a regular payment financed by the mortgage. A mortgage-backed security is many of these bonds packaged together, the idea being that diversifying mortgage holders reduces the risk from someone defaulting or paying back the mortgage early.* Pullman figured he could do something similar with Bowie's music income.

The timing couldn't have been better. Bowie and Pullman made a deal with EMI to rerelease the twenty-five albums made between 1969 and 1990. Bowie was guaranteed more than 25 percent of the royalties from wholesale sales in the United States. Bowie's catalog was valued at about $100 million, an income stream ripe for hedging. Pullman proposed securitizing Bowie's royalties.

Bowie loved the idea; he would get money now and he'd still technically own his music, but the money his royalties generated would go to someone else for fifteen years. Pullman says after he described how it would work, Bowie quickly asked, "Why haven't we started this yet?"

The deal came together in a few months and there was no shortage of potential buyers. Before the deal was completed, rumors of it leaked out and Pullman was flooded with calls. The Bowie Bond, as it was known, was attractive to insurance companies, which have to make regular payments to their beneficiaries years into the future. Owning a long-term bond, like a Bowie Bond, is how they hedge risk, because they need an asset that offers a regular stream of payouts.

Prudential paid $55 million and in exchange got a 7.9 percent interest payment on their principal for fifteen years.† These interest payments were financed by the income generated by royalties from Bowie's albums recorded before 1990. If for some reason the music did not generate enough revenue (and exhausted a reserve fund), Bowie's catalog would be owned by Prudential. But that did not happen, since the income from music royalties is fairly stable for older artists with established catalogs.

This was a hedge because Bowie took $55 million to forgo his royalty

---

* Though, as we saw in the financial crisis of 2008, diversification did not reduce the systematic risk that lots of people would default at the same time.
† Similar to prepaying a mortgage, if the income generated by the royalties was greater than expected, they would pay out more and pay off the bond early.

payments for fifteen years. He got less upside by giving them up in exchange for the certainty of $55 million up front. Perhaps Bowie was less inclined to take risk when he was older, or maybe he saw more risk ahead with a changing music industry. Either way, he decided to hedge.

BUY SOMETHING THAT GOES UP WHEN ANOTHER THING GOES DOWN

Instead of buying a risk-free asset as a hedge, you could buy two different assets that move in opposite directions. Think of betting against your football team: the loss of one outcome (feeling badly that your team lost) is offset by a gain (getting money when your team loses). Or suppose you are captain of a cruise ship. When the cruise industry does well you get paid more: there are more trips and people pay more for cruises, which increases your pay. But if there's another "poop cruise" incident, demand might fall, leading to fewer trips and lower fares, meaning lower pay or even the threat of losing your job. A cruise ship captain can hedge poop-cruise risk by investing in hotels or land-based resorts or other companies that profit when cruises are unpopular.

NEGATIVE HEDGE: MORE RISK, MORE REWARD

Hedging is a strategy that reduces risk, but like any risk strategy, it can be flipped around to increase both risk and expected payoffs. Suppose you want an extra rush when watching a football game. You could take a negative hedge and increase risk by betting on your own team. If you win, you are doubly happy: you get both bragging rights and money. If you lose, you face double disappointment: your team's a dud and you drop some cash.

One hedging technique is to lend money to the government, a company, or a city by buying a bond that promises to pay you a certain amount for a prespecified time. Because the amount the bond pays is fixed, it is less risky than owning a stock, which means there's less risk in your portfolio.* Shifting out of a risky investment like stocks and combining them with bonds can be a hedge.

The opposite strategy is *borrowing* money and using it to make a risky investment; this is called leverage, and it is a negative hedge. It is how people magnify risk and is often at the root of financial crises. Donald learned this lesson when he borrowed money from his father to fund his candy scheme. He made money until his supply suddenly disappeared, and he couldn't pay back his father.

Here's another example of leverage. The post office sells Forever Stamps, which retain their value even if the price of stamps goes up. Suppose you knew the price of postage stamps was set to increase from 45 to 50 cents next week. If you buy a Forever Stamp this week for 45 cents, it will be worth 50 cents next week. This knowledge presents an opportunity.

Imagine you have $10,000 and spend it all on Forever Stamps. The day after the price increase you sell the 22,222 stamps for $11,111. You'd make $1,111, an 11 percent return in just a few days.

That's not bad, but you can do better if you take on more risk. Say you borrow another $90,000 from a bank by taking out a second mortgage on your house at a 5 percent (monthly) interest rate. You take the loan and your savings and buy $100,000 worth of stamps. If you sell them all in a month you'd get $111,111. After paying back the bank loan plus a month's worth of interest ($94,500), you have a profit of $6,611. That's nearly six times what you'd get if you self-financed the postage stamp arbitrage.

Obviously, this is a very risky bet. There's a good chance you can't sell

---

* Assuming the entity that issues the bond doesn't default and pays you back.

222,222 stamps in a month. If after a few months, you still can't sell them, the interest payments will eat away all your profits. And if you can never sell them, you'll lose your home. Taking on leverage is the kind of high risk/high reward transaction that makes some people in finance superrich (if they are lucky) and destroys the careers of others (and even whole economies).

The stamp story may sound like a crazy risk to take, but equally outlandish bets are placed every day. Leverage explains the high returns many hedge funds manage to achieve each year. Most of the time, people who seem to get more aren't performing any great magic or aren't smarter than the rest of us. They just take more risk.

HEDGING THE FUTURE OF CRUISING

Donald took a big risk shortly after becoming CEO that will define his legacy at Carnival. A year after he joined, Carnival poached John Padgett from Disney. Padgett is the brains behind the Disney MagicBand, an electronic band guests wear at Disney parks that tracks where they are to coordinate their transportation and cut down on line waiting times.

Padgett and his team came up with a similar product for Carnival, the Ocean Medallion. It takes the MagicBand idea a step further. Cruising can be impersonal and generic. You get an easy vacation that does not require you to think or plan, but you're also one of a herd of three thousand people—that's the risk trade-off. The Medallion promises to offer the best of both worlds. It simulates a more personalized experience: cruise staff are told your name and what you like to eat or drink before you enter shipboard restaurants or bars. The technology anticipates what activities you'd enjoy; for example, sipping a Martini last night might mean you'd be interested in snorkeling today. The Medallion constantly updates data to anticipate your every need and desire, even before you want something—an Orwellian cruise experience.

Taking on this technology is a risk. Retraining the staff and rewiring the ships are essential. Negatives include a high likelihood of glitches early on, the high cost of implementing the technology, and customers' unease with sharing data. The Medallion was announced at the 2017 Consumer Electronics Show, where it was lauded as the new future of cruising and received lots of media coverage. But what was not mentioned was Donald's careful hedging strategy: go big and then be careful.

The Medallion was rolled out *very* slowly. Several months after the announcement a handful of select passengers got to try it on a single cruise ship on the premium Princess Line. It was more than a year before all the passengers on the ship could use it. As of 2018, Medallion access on all Carnival ships was estimated to be years away. When I told Padgett I interviewed Donald about risk hedging, he said, "Well, Arnold is a master of *that*. If you look at this particular innovation effort [the Medallion], it has its risks, but he keeps everything in perspective. The biggest bet is one percent of our fleet, [and] it's betting in a way that has almost no downside."

Donald's success comes down to hard work, intellect, and combining big expectations with prudence. He expects the best and plans for the worst. This strategy may lack the drama behind the vaunted achievements of other famous businesspeople, but it increases the odds of success.

Chapter 10

INSURANCE:
Introducing the Spectacular Stock Option

Fun is like life insurance; the older you get, the more it costs.

—FRANK MCKINNEY "KIN" HUBBARD, AMERICAN CARTOONIST, HUMORIST, AND JOURNALIST

The word "insurance" does not normally conjure feelings of excitement. Often we think of agents in ill-fitting suits selling life insurance, or an actuary working in a windowless room calculating when we might die. But insurance does something wondrous: it reduces the cost of a risk gone wrong, while allowing us to enjoy the upside of risk taking. With hedging we must give up the gains if things go better than expected, but with insurance we get to keep them. This is why, in many ways, insurance can seem just like magic.

Ten times a week in a dark and dingy apartment in the thick of the Hell's Kitchen neighborhood of New York City, Belinda Sinclair performs magic too. On the day I am there, her audience is fewer than twelve people. She serves tea and connects with everyone, picking up on their thoughts, desires, and skepticism and tailoring her distinctly feminine show to their personality.

One of a few female magicians who perform shows, she describes the noble history of women in magic. We usually associate magic with men, but women have a long, underappreciated contribution to the dark arts. Often it was women who worked as healers and mystics, mixing potions and telling fortunes. In nineteenth-century New York, women hosted small gatherings like Sinclair's in their parlors and performed magic tricks. It was around the time of Houdini when men were associated with performing illusions for large audiences and women were relegated to the assistant role.

Sinclair says we are drawn to magic because it suggests humans have powers that give them order and control in a world that is often harsh and unpredictable. A magician can defy the cruel randomness of nature. Believing in magic suggests there are humans who have the ability to control gravity, time, space, and even death. If they can do it, perhaps we all can too, or we can pay for the services of someone who possesses these special gifts.

Of course, this order is an illusion, a con. Conning is what magicians do and what you pay to experience. They make you feel comfortable and trusting, then they do something that appears to defy all laws of gravity and human consciousness. It is no coincidence that successful magicians tend to be both strange and exceedingly likable. Pulling off a magic trick requires fooling your target, and that means directing what they see and feel. Sinclair achieves that by being totally attuned to her audience's every emotion. When you interact with other people, they usually aren't so aware of your emotions most of the time, because they are invested in what they need to get out of the interaction. When someone is so aware of you and your needs, he or she has power over you and you feel safe and trusting. This is what magicians need from their audience.

Sinclair's parlor is tricked out with mirrors and wires, and she seats her audience strategically by height so she has some control over what they see. She is constantly observing everyone, like the middle-aged man whose face lights up like a small boy's when she retrieves the card he printed his name on. She wins over the hardened skeptic dragged there by his wife when she makes a coin float above his palm. She plants words in your head and then guesses the one you're thinking of.

Sinclair speaks with a warm affect; in her midfifties, she has the complexion of a thirty-five-year-old, her face framed by very long, graying, curly hair. It is no surprise she was a model in her youth. Sinclair has had many careers. She still lives within a few blocks of where she grew up in New York City, surrounded by a large extended family.

Sinclair was a child actor and went to a performing arts high school. But after college, she aspired to become a doctor and studied medicine. Part of her training included working with sick children in a hospital. One day the hospital asked Sinclair to put on a show for the kids since she had a background in theater and clowning. She was such a hit that a parent offered her $100 to come to her house for her child's birthday party.

Sensing a regular source of income to supplement her studies, Sinclair went to a local magic shop to buy supplies, where she found many of the tricks overpriced and not very good. The men at the shop dared her to do better, so she went home and made her first trick, which she won't reveal. The magic men were so impressed with her artistry they offered Sinclair work illustrating their catalog, which included all the tricks they sold and drawings of how they worked. After five years of illustrating, Sinclair gained an encyclopedic knowledge of how magic tricks work: "I learned firsthand . . . how the eye works when it sees a trick, how the hand works, how the redirect works. . . . Magic forces you to stop, observe, and anticipate how the client reacts. There is an art to being prepared for action and reaction."

She eventually dropped out of medical school and used her

background in theater to start working with magicians and producing their stage shows. When she was twenty-nine, Sinclair started her own magic act.

She practices close-up magic that includes card and coin tricks. Sinclair is confident enough in her sleight-of-hand skills that she explains to me how she can pick a particular card out of a deck. Because holding the card makes it warmer than the others, it bends ever so slightly, so she can find it in the deck. Another tip: it takes at least seven shuffles to change the order of most cards, so she asks her guests to shuffle three times. Learning and performing each trick can take more than a year of practice. It requires a certain dexterity of the hand; for each trick, Sinclair builds up her hand muscles to palm the card just so.

When I ask her if tricks go wrong, Sinclair gives me a sly smile and says, "All the time." But her tricks don't fail.

"At that point you *redirect,*" she says. "It is not really conning—it is redirecting their attention. If I can't find the card, I hand the deck back to them and say, 'Check the deck; make sure your card is still there.' The key word is 'still.'"

The audience thinks this step is part of the act, but it gives Sinclair the opportunity to figure out where the card is. All that practice and years of study ultimately come down to mastering a backup plan to make sure the trick goes well. No matter what it is—a mirror in the corner, distracting your audience for a second, or redirecting—having that extra insurance in your back pocket can save a show. A single flop can destroy the trust that is necessary to pull off an illusion.

Sinclair's most critical skill isn't her deep knowledge of magic or her ability to palm a card; rather, it is her ability to save any trick and still awe the audience even if things go wrong. All successful magicians must master the art of the save. Some will even share how their tricks are done. But the secret they all keep is how they insure themselves. For Sinclair, in a small room, up close, where her audience can see anything, the time and energy she spends attending to you so you trust her before she redirects is her insurance.

INSURANCE IS MAGIC

Insurance works like magic. It reduces your risk, just like hedging does, but with one important difference. With hedging you must take less risk; you give up the extra upside of your potential reward in exchange for lessening the risk that something goes horribly wrong. If you risk less, you get less. Insurance appears to pull off the unimaginable: downside protection with unlimited upside.

For example, suppose you decide to become a commercial crab fisherman, one of the world's most dangerous jobs. The odds of getting killed or disabled are much higher than they are for accountants. But all the risk can pay off. You can make up to $50,000 a month during crab season, more than most accountants get paid in a year. Hedging risk in this case would be avoiding the most dangerous fishing areas, like the Bering Sea, which has the roughest weather and also the biggest crabs. You take on less risk and also give up the potential for big earnings; maybe you make only $30,000 a month instead of $50,000 but you reduce the risk of being maimed or killed.

Insurance deals with risk in a different way. You buy life or disability insurance because providing for your family matters most to you. If something bad happens to you on the dangerous seas, your family will still have income, but at the same time you preserve the potential to reap big returns in the most perilous waters.

You can insure just about anything you can imagine: your house, your life, your ability to work, your car, or your vacation. A model can even insure her legs; Dolly Parton insured her breasts. These are all examples of someone else taking on another person's risk for a price.

But this security is not free. You pay someone else a premium, and in exchange they take on your downside risk. The upside is still yours, minus the cost of the insurance premium. And just as with magic, people are often skeptical of what they are paying for. They might doubt the premium is worth the protection; some may even think they are being conned.

Often insurance is a good deal. Like magic, insurance can make some risk disappear. That's because transferring risk to an insurance company is efficient. Suppose a model wants to insure against breaking her leg and losing months of income. If she self-insured, she'd need to put aside all that lost income, just in case something bad happens, because she bears all that risk on her own. But if she buys insurance, she only has to pay an insurance company a fraction of that lost income because it sells the same policy to hundreds of other models, and most of them won't ever need their insurance since the odds of breaking a leg are pretty low. This is how insurance companies diversify risk: they pool all the premiums the models pay together and use this money to pay for that one unlucky model who will need to make a claim. The risk is reduced, though not eliminated. Say there is a freak accident at a fashion show and more than one model breaks her leg. The insurance company must bear the tail risk and compensate the injured models for their lost income.

Buying insurance is more efficient than bearing the risk ourselves. But when there is no market for our risk, we find a way to insure ourselves in our daily lives. Paying a price for a contingency plan is a form of insurance, whether it's putting down a deposit for an alternate location if your wedding is rained out or carrying the weight of extra water on a hike in case you get lost and dehydrated.

Sinclair cannot buy insurance against a magic trick failing. Perhaps one day magicians will form an alliance and rescue one another's tricks, but that day is not here yet. So instead Sinclair has devoted years to learning how to connect with her audience and control what they see so she is able to save her tricks if something goes wrong. Her time spent honing the skill to rescue tricks and the trust she builds with her audience are her insurance. She can enjoy the unlimited benefits of a great magic show without the worry of tricks failing.

Even if we can't buy it, commercial insurance, in addition to reducing risk, serves another important function. Insurance policies are bought and sold. In order for these transactions to happen, the value of eliminating downside risk needs a price. Even if we don't buy insurance, the price helps us gauge risk and understand which situations are riskier than others.

OPTIONS

There is insurance on financial assets too. You can pay someone a premium to insure against the price of a stock falling too far. This kind of insurance is a financial instrument called a stock option, a contract stipulating you can buy or sell a stock for a certain price within a few months or years, depending on the terms. For example, if you buy a put option, you pay a premium and someone promises you can sell them stock at a particular price in the future. Suppose you buy Facebook stock for $200 a share. You are optimistic about the company's future but a little worried that it shares stories from dubious news sources, which might pose a risk that the stock price will fall one day. You can buy a put option that gives you the right to sell Facebook for $150 any time during the next six months. A put option offers insurance against the chance that Facebook's stock price will tank.

Here's another example: If you buy a call option, you pay a premium and someone promises you can *buy* a stock for a certain price in the future, no matter what the market price turns out to be. Say it's the day after the 2016 U.S. election. The new president's preferred method of communication is Twitter, so you anticipate a Trump victory will make it a more valuable company. You think the price of Twitter stock will go up from $19 to $40 in the next six months but don't want to make a financial commitment to that prediction just yet. You could buy a call option for $2 that guarantees you can purchase Twitter stock for just $30. Six months from now you plan on exercising your option, buying Twitter for $30 and then selling it for $40 and making a nice profit.

Of course, no one knows what will happen six months from now. By April 10, 2017, the price of Twitter stock fell to $14.30 a share and it never got above $26 that year. If your option was only good for six months, it turned out to be worthless; you paid $2 for nothing. Investors use put and call options to make bets on what will happen to the stock market.

Options reduce risk by offering a payoff if a certain thing happens, just like insurance offers you money if your house burns down or you break a leg. In the same spirit, options deliver money when a specified event happens, like a stock price falling or rising (depending on the contract). If you insure against a stock price falling, you reduce the risk of losing money but still get the unlimited benefit of the stock price going up, minus what you paid for the premium you paid for the option.

Options are a form of insurance, but if you own one you don't have to exercise it. The option may be to sell or buy a stock at a certain price before the specified date, pay your mortgage back early, or even keep dating your partner without committing to marriage. You don't have to make a commitment now—for a small fee you can wait and see what happens before you act. And there is no cost to waiting (perhaps your partner will get fed up, but you'll still have your stock portfolio to keep you warm at night) because you are certain to buy or sell at the price in your options contract, no matter what happens to the actual price.

You can use options just like hedging or any other risk reduction strategy to amplify rather than reduce risk. For example, you can bet big on an upswing in the stock market and take on more leverage to enhance your wager. If you're wrong, you can end up losing even more than if you'd just bought shares of a single stock that crashed.

Maybe you decide to take a chance on Twitter stock going from $19 to

$40 in the next six months. Instead of buying one share of the stock, you could buy ten call options for $2 each, which gives you the right to buy Twitter stock for $30 anytime in the next six months. If the price does go to $40, you'll make $80 ($80 = ($40 – $30)*10 – $20). That's much more than the $21 you'd make if you just bought one share of Twitter, but there is also more risk. If the price falls to $17, your call options are worthless, and you lose the full $20 you spent on them. If you bought one share of the stock, you would have lost only $2. Options can magnify gains and losses, similar to borrowing money to make a risky bet.

Most people assume financial derivatives like options are a modern invention that has infected markets and made them riskier. But options have been traded for thousands of years, and people have been wary of them just as long. Aristotle, who thought poorly of people who chased wealth, wrote disapprovingly of how the philosopher Thales made a killing by buying options on olive presses when he anticipated a good harvest.

In the past, it was hard to put a price on how much we valued risk. This changed in the 1970s, when the finance professors Fischer Black and Myron Scholes developed a formula to price options. Around the same time, Robert C. Merton, another finance professor, came up with a robust way to solve for an option's price. His model offered a quick, objective way to price risk based on a few characteristics that were easy to observe and measure.

At first, their work on options pricing seemed like another academic curiosity with lots of esoteric math, but the papers written on the Black-Scholes model and its solution turned out to be some of the most influential financial research ever published. People traded options before the 1970s, but they tended to be created for specific transactions, in the same way Thales approached the owners of olive presses looking to make a deal. But the world had become a riskier place and the demand for insurance had grown, so this method wouldn't cut it much longer. As the economy grew and became more interconnected, there was more demand for ways to insure against the risk of investing in foreign markets. Demand also grew because the world became riskier, the certain exchange rates from the Bretton Woods agreement* were no more, and oil prices and inflation had spiked. More individuals and institutions were seeking ways to deal with this risk. The options market needed a reliable, consistent, and replicable way to price risk in order for it to grow to meet the new demand.

Coincidentally, soon after Black, Scholes, and Merton published their papers, the Chicago Board of Trade started an exchange on which options could be bought and sold in large volume. The Black-Scholes model provided pricing everyone could agree on. As it happened, at the same time, advancements in electronic calculators made it possible for the model to be programmed into traders' calculators. In 1973, the first day the exchange was in operation, only 911[†] call options changed hands. A year later, the average daily volume had grown to 20,000 contracts traded, and by 2016, on average more than 4 million options contracts changed hands each day on just that one exchange.[‡]

The price of insurance can tell us how risky a situation is, but how can we know if the price of insurance is worth it or if we are being conned? By helping us to better understand what makes one situation riskier than another, the Black-Scholes model is a tool we can use to distinguish a bargain from a trick.

THE GREEKS KNOW RISK

The price of an option (a put or a call) depends on only four different parameters. How much each of these factors matters can tell us a lot

---

* A fixed exchange rate regime that collapsed in 1973; after that, exchange rates floated in the market and became more uncertain.
† At first, only call options were traded.
‡ Dozens of other exchanges have opened all over the world.

about how much risk we face. In the Black-Scholes model these relationships are called the Greeks.

1. Vega: More Volatility, More Risk

The first thing you should look at is the range of possibilities. Chapter 4 described risk measurement, the range of things that might happen. We generally focus our risk concerns on the range of things that are most probable, called volatility. The bigger this range is, the more risk we face. And generally, the larger your volatility is, the more you have to give up to protect yourself from bad outcomes.

The riskier any situation is, the more we must pay to insure ourselves. If there is construction on the highway to the airport, the range of possible travel times is bigger, and we need to budget more time to get there.

2. Delta: Odds You'll Be in the Money

Next you need to worry about the odds something will go wrong. Even if you compare two scenarios with the same amount of volatility, sometimes one is more likely to need insurance than the other. And the more likely you are to need insurance, the more expensive it is.

Hurricane insurance costs more for a house in Florida than it does in Arizona because Floridians are more likely to need this kind of insurance. Insurance companies charge high-risk customers more—people who are more likely to be sicker or to drive recklessly, or companies that don't practice good cyber hygiene. The commercial fisherman in the Bering Sea will pay bigger life insurance premiums than an accountant will.

The last time you bought an airline ticket, odds are you also sold an option and didn't even realize it. As discussed in chapter 1, airlines reserve the option of kicking you off the plane if the flight is overbooked. The lower your fare class, or the cheaper your ticket, the higher you are on the list to be bumped off your flight. Your cheap ticket is so cheap, in part, because you sold an option to take a later flight if the plane is full. The more likely you are to be bumped, the more valuable the option is to the airline, so the bigger the discount on your plane ticket.

3. Theta: The Value of Time

Another consideration is how long the risk will last. Is there a risk of something going wrong for the next month or the next year? The longer you are at risk, the more risk you face. And the longer an insurance contract covers you for, the more expensive it is. There is a common misconception that the more time you have before the risk is realized, the less risky it is.

For example, you are often told it's less risky to invest in stocks when you are young because if the stock market drops you have years to make it up. This is what financial economists call the "fallacy of time diversification" because that assumption is wrong. It is true there's a good chance the market will recover in a decade or two; often time will wipe out a big loss. But that does not necessarily mean there's less risk, because twenty years of investing means there's also the possibility of twenty years of bad returns. If you are only investing for two years, that possibility doesn't exist. Depending on how you look at it, a longer time in the market can mean more risk.

The same is true if you hope to increase the odds of being happily married. Women face pressure to marry young or get "left on the shelf." But your odds of finding someone to marry remain high well into middle age (and even beyond), and your odds of getting divorced fall dramatically the older you are when you marry. That's not only because you have fewer years of marriage when things can go wrong but also because people who marry older are more stable and fully formed. Marrying young is a risk. You'll have more financial stress, and the person you marry may grow into a different person.

4. Rho: Risk-Free Rate

Often taking a risk is a choice. You can sit at home and watch Netflix on a rainy night, or you can go on a blind date. How appealing the safe option is matters. Before Netflix, TV choices were more limited. You might be more inclined to go out no matter what because staying in wasn't so tempting. Now, thanks to streaming, the risk-free option is better, and the dating stakes are higher. How much we value risk—and, by extension, how much we are willing to pay to reduce it—often depends on what the safe alternative offers.

In finance, the value of a safe asset plays many important roles in the pricing of assets and derivatives. It is how much you earn without taking on any risk at all. There is no need to take a risk if the no- or low-risk option is almost as good. In this case, taking a risk is just not worth it. Risk-free also represents how much it costs to finance a risky bet (recall the 5 percent second-mortgage interest rate in the postage stamp arbitrage in chapter 9).

This value of the safe option also drives many aspects of risky decision making. For example, it explains why some economists now believe mass incarceration may have caused more crime than it prevented. You'd think putting more people in prison would *reduce* crime. After all, we are taking criminals off the street. But mass incarceration went too far and sent many nonviolent offenders to prison. Even if you are a lightweight criminal, going to prison can change you. You learn lawbreaking skills and gain connections in the criminal world. Once you get out of prison you have more opportunities in crime.

What really matters is that the safe option—staying away from crime—is less valuable than it was before you went to prison. Once you are released, your options in the legal world are limited. It's hard to get a job if you are a convicted felon.

Or to put it another way, crime can be even more attractive after you've been in prison, especially when compared with a law-abiding life, the risk-free choice. This explains, in part, why about 76 percent of criminals reoffend.

INSURANCE IS MAGIC WITH CONTRACTS

In almost all practical ways, magic is very different from insurance. Magic is an illusion, a con, and insurance contracts are legal documents. If you get into a car accident, or a stock price falls below a certain level, or another insurable event happens, you aren't left hanging the way you would be in the middle of a magic trick gone wrong. Someone is legally obligated to pay you.

Despite what many people assume, insurance cheats you only some of the time. Magic always cheats you, which is what you expect when you go to a magic show. Many people are wary of insurance contracts because sometimes they are complicated, expensive, and opaque, like the option you unwittingly sold on your plane seat. The terms of your options contract are hidden in your ticket's small print. Odds are you'll be angry, and rightly so, if you are involuntarily bumped and physically dragged off the plane.

Simple life annuity contracts are another powerful and valuable risk mitigation tool (see the discussion in chapter 3); they are insurance against living for a long time. No matter how long you live, an insurance company pays you. They can even increase your spending in retirement because you pool your risk with that of other retirees. If you are afraid of outliving your savings, this can be extremely valuable insurance. Unfortunately, some types of annuities, often peddled by third-party brokers, got a bad name on account of fees hidden in the fine print.

Insurance contracts have many variants, and when the world of risk gets more complicated, so do contracts. Many offer valuable risk protection, but some contracts aren't worth the paper they are printed on, let alone the large premium you pay.

As a consumer, you must ask two questions when you buy insurance:

1. What does the insurance cover exactly?

   What is your goal, and are you actually insuring against something that threatens it? Often it is tempting to buy insurance to cover a risk we aren't worried about or one we are already insured against; for example, buying insurance for a car rental when we already have credit card insurance, or buying insurance in case our TV falls off the wall when we keep it on a stand.

2. How much does it cost?

   We can use the Greeks from the Black-Scholes model to figure out if the value of insurance is worth paying a premium: Are you facing a high-risk situation? What are the odds you'll need insurance? How long does the policy last? How much would you save if you avoided risk instead?

ARE OPTIONS AN ILLUSION?

Since the 2008 financial crisis, financial derivatives and the models like Black-Scholes that facilitate them have been widely criticized. One critique is that there is no reliable way to price risk and the model creates a false comfort that emboldens risk taking. Like one of Sinclair's tricks, it's all an illusion.

Magic is an illusion that appears to suggest humans have control over the cruel randomness of nature. Some would say the same of options pricing, and there are parallels. Robert K. Merton, the father of Robert C., was a very serious amateur magician who dreamed of being a professional. The name Merton was Robert K.'s adopted stage name, a play on Merlin; the original family name is Schkolnick. A magic career didn't work out for Merton senior. Instead, he became a renowned sociologist; "self-fulfilling prophecy" and "unintended consequences" are two of the well-known concepts he developed. Aspects of Merton's theories are relevant for understanding risk pricing.

Sinclair believes that magic, even if it is an illusion, unlocks people's potential: "It opens up a sense of wonder. Our potential is greater than we think it is." The wonder you experience in a magic show can propel you to take more risk and realize you are truly capable of bigger things. The magic becomes a self-fulfilling prophecy if it unlocks a sense of possibility and bolsters your confidence to rise to your potential, enabling something that usually wouldn't happen to become possible. In some sense, the magic becomes real. Sinclair explains, "I make [people] feel confident, comfortable, and safe. Then they can enjoy and play; if they feel better about themselves, then magic has happened."

Of course, that magic never existed, and in the same way there may be no true price of risk. Options pricing is merely an estimate of risk in an uncertain market. But the fact that risk price is never a precise truth misses the point of risk models and any price derived from them. Any map is inaccurate because it does not include every small road and tree, but that does not make the map worthless. Its purpose is to direct you by helping you to understand how certain features relate to each other. That is also what a financial model like Black-Scholes does: it offers a consistent, transparent, easy-to-use method to understand how different factors—current price, volatility, time—relate to the price of risk in a way everyone can understand and agree on. That's what makes it so valuable. Once everyone agrees on how prices are to be calculated and uses the same model, the price is deemed to be right, which creates some order in a chaotic market.

An aura of magic surrounds financial options. In the worlds of both magic and finance, a sense of control can embolden us to take more risk.

Taking more risk can be positive; it is how we move forward in life and achieve great things. Options are insurance contracts, and insurance can give us a sense of security, but sometimes that means we take on more risk than we should.

That's not all. Risk-reducing technologies like options can be flipped around to amplify risk. For example, options can be used to make bets on the stock market, creating more risk instead of cutting it. People in the financial industry often use options to take more risk instead of reducing it.

The trade-off between risk and security is tricky, but on balance the insurance provided by financial derivatives reduces most risk; however, if a systematic blowup like the Great Recession occurs, the cost can be steep (though, thankfully, infrequent).

Chapter 11

MORAL HAZARDS:
Surfing Big Waves with Insurance

*Only those who will risk going too far can possibly
find out how far one can go.*

—T. S. ELIOT

A safety net can either catch you when you fall or be used as a sling-shot to propel you to new heights. Not only that, the fact that the safety net is there may embolden you to take bigger risks. This doesn't mean we should get rid of safety nets, but we do need to be thoughtful about how we use risk management tools. This is not a conversation people like to have in finance or government; it is easier to blame excessive risk taking on the safety net instead of the person who used it in a reckless way.

I went to Oahu's North Shore seeking a community whose members take a more productive approach to the downsides of risk management: big wave surfers. Their lives depend on using risk management techniques, even though those same tools also expose them to bigger risks.

G reg Long says he's a control freak. Control freak is not how you'd usually describe someone who seems so cool—Long is a champion big wave surfer, born and bred on the beaches of Southern

California—or someone who, when you finally track him down, tells you he was camping on the beach in Mexico for a few weeks, far away from a phone signal.

Big wave surfers are a different breed from regular surfers. Instead of surfing smaller waves at well-attended competitions at highly trafficked beaches, big wave surfers seek out waves that are 20 to 80 feet high—the height of buildings—often in remote locations. Long is renowned in the surfing community not only for being one the best big wave riders of his generation but also for his fanatical approach to managing risk.

Long surfed his first big wave when he was fifteen off the coast of Baja California with his father, a lifeguard, and his older brother. His father taught him to never go into the water without a safety plan, the latest gear, and a thorough knowledge of the conditions.

In the popular imagination, big wave surfers are daredevils, thrill seekers who mindlessly chase the biggest wave they can find. This does not describe Long or any of the big wave surfers I met.

"I was never an adrenaline junkie," Long explains to me. "Maybe when I was younger, but it was mostly [about a particular] wave, a huge force of energy, and the challenge of figuring out where I had to be to ride it, and learning each time how I could do it better next time."

Finding the right wave is not easy. It is not simply a matter of wave size since the ultimate wave must meet several conditions: the wind must be just so, the energy of the swell high enough, and the distance between two successive waves optimal. Knowing this information before you get in the water can be the difference between life and death. Gone are the days when surfers spot a large wave out their window, call their friends, and surf it. Long is a self-taught meteorologist and has developed personal relationships with professional weather forecasters. He scours data on surf conditions around the world looking for where the ideal conditions will be—the California coast, Tahiti, Hawaii, South Africa, Portugal, Ireland.

Oceans and weather are like financial markets: controlled chaos. You can plan and manage risk, but things can always go wrong. This happened to Long on December 21, 2012, one hundred miles off the coast of Southern California. Typical of Long, he'd left little to chance. He knew the conditions and had the latest safety gear. As on any of his expeditions, Long traveled with a large group, including a dedicated rescue team. For this trip, that meant six men on jet skis. It's not unusual for surfers to be accompanied by an entourage of photographers, and Long's were all trained water professionals in their own right, also on jet skis and able to perform a rescue if necessary.

Long wiped out on the second wave of a five-wave set and was dragged deep underwater. He activated the inflatable vest he was wearing by pulling a tab. The vest failed to inflate and bring him to the surface; Long was stranded underwater as massive waves barreled above him.

Long remained calm. He had trained for this type of emergency; he can hold his breath for five and a half minutes. Long had to make a decision: swim to the top for air and rescue or wait for the third wave in the set to pass. Waiting out the next wave would be more prudent; swimming to the surface would burn precious energy and oxygen. If he tried to surface as the wave was breaking, the force would prevent him from reaching air. But Long was running out of oxygen and anxious to get to the top. He decided to go for it. The next wave was already upon him as he approached the surface and, a mere 2 feet from the air, Long was pushed back down 30 feet. The force of the third wave shook the remaining breath from his lungs and he went into a state of shock. His body convulsed and he fought every instinct to start breathing and inhale water.

With zero oxygen, Long used his last burst of energy and grabbed on to the leash around his ankle that tethered him to his board. He climbed his leash up to his board, which was at that point submerged 10 feet below the surface.

Cramping, numbness, and full-body convulsions returned. Long couldn't get a solid grasp on his board and lost consciousness as the fourth wave passed above him. Thankfully, he was still attached to his board, which had floated to the surface. Another surfer working rescue that day, DK Walsh, spotted Long's board, dove in, and saved him. Long was placed on a sled attached to a rescue jet ski and taken to the expedition's boat moored nearby.

Long regained consciousness once he got to the boat. Still in shock, he coughed up foamy blood and was given oxygen before being airlifted to a hospital, where he made a quick physical recovery. Within days he was back in the lineup surfing Mavericks in Northern California, though the experience still haunts him. "Riding big waves used to fill my dreams in the most blissful way," he told *Surfing Magazine*. "Now they came in the form of nightmares."

BIG WAVE SURFERS ARE JUST LIKE ACTUARIES, ONLY WITH BETTER TANS

You might not think a big wave surfer and a financial engineer have much in common. But they both face the same problem: insurance removes the downside and leaves us with unlimited upside, but that gives us the incentive and the ability to take even bigger risks.

This is one big reason why people are wary of modern finance. Regulators struggle to rein in excessive risk taking, while still getting the benefits from risk mitigation tools that aim to make markets less risky. But they aren't the only ones who search for the right balance.

I went searching for answers at a risk conference for big wave surfers. Now, risk conferences are usually my domain (I am a retirement economist after all), so it was a little strange at first to see the surfers out of their natural habitat in a neon-lit hotel conference room with only one small window. In many ways the Big Wave Risk Assessment Group

(BWRAG) Safety Summit on the North Shore of Oahu was different from other risk conferences I've attended. Everyone (but me) was tan and in excellent physical shape—even participants well into their sixties. Most wore shorts, T-shirts, and flip-flops. The day included workshops on holding your breath led by deep-sea divers. Former Special Forces officers instructed us on how to tie a tourniquet and perform an emergency tracheotomy with a pen. At one point, someone used the word "gnarly," but as a technical term. I even renewed my CPR certification.

But in other ways, the Big Wave Safety Summit was just like a pension risk conference: most of the attendees were men; a majority of the time was spent looking at PowerPoint slides of numbers and figures; and there were impassioned debates about who bears responsibility for risk regulation. Surfers also shared the latest tools on how to minimize risk and discussed techniques on how to turn uncertainty into risk by estimating probabilities.*

The goal of the conference is to apply risk science to big wave surfing. Instead of going into the ocean and hoping for the best, surfers are schooled in the "art" of risk: how to form calculated, informed risk assessments. The risk mitigation tools appear to be different from those used in financial markets, but they serve a similar purpose. Surfers form well-trained teams to raise the odds of a successful rescue (diversification). They monitor wave conditions, identify hazards (sharks, crowds, rocks, deep water, cold), and make probability estimates on the odds things will go wrong. This is so the surfers can make informed trade-offs about the thrill of riding a big wave safely (hedging). And they use the latest technology to rescue them when they wipe out (insurance).

Some of the techniques are low-tech and commonsense. For example, waves tend to travel in packs, or sets. If you know the surfable waves in front of you are part of a five-wave set, a hedging strategy is taking

---

* Shout-out to Gerd Gigerenzer: the surfers were encouraged to think in terms of frequencies instead of pure probabilities.

the fourth wave, even if the first one is bigger. That way after you finish, or wipe out, you aren't pounded or held underwater by the next big waves in the set. Long says he usually takes later waves in a set. That day in 2012 was an exception. He had been out in the water for more than four hours and had already let lots of great waves pass only to find the later waves in the set small or unsurfable. That second wave he took was part of the first large five-wave set that day.

The Big Wave Safety Summit started after the famed surfer Sion Milosky drowned off the coast of Northern California. Surfers decided there needed to be more safety and training mechanisms in place and best practices established to reduce risk. BWRAG brings surfers together to make safety a priority and learn about the latest risk technology.

Risk awareness is more critical than before as technology continues to transform big wave surfing. A sport of a few men riding 20- to 30-foot waves has morphed into a scientific endeavor, supported by the latest gadgets, to surf 50-, even 80-foot waves. When used correctly, technology augments but does not replace skill. The problem is many surfers use technology to make up for deficient swimming and surfing abilities.

BROTHERS FROM ANOTHER MOTHER

Brian Keaulana is one of the founders of BWRAG. He is to big wave surfing what Robert C. Merton is to finance. Merton enabled the widespread use of options to financial markets, which empowered people to take risks in markets by having insurance against downside. Keaulana introduced jet skis to big wave surfing; these invaluable tools are used to rescue surfers who wipe out. A jet ski saved Greg Long's life.

Jet skis can cut through rough waters so an injured surfer can be brought to shore quickly to receive medical attention. They are effectively insurance: providing protection if things go wrong, while still offering the unlimited upside of surfing big waves.

Keaulana is in his midfifties, a lifelong Hawaiian big wave surfer, former lifeguard, and now noted stuntman. He played himself in an episode of *Baywatch*. Keaulana speaks proudly of Hawaiian values of knowing and respecting the water. He marries his spirituality and reverence for tradition with a love of technology and a fierce interest in modern risk strategy. He proudly showed off his latest Apple Watch and explained that it is waterproof so he can make phone calls when he is in the ocean to coordinate a rescue.

Just like Merton, Keaulana was profoundly influenced by his father, Richard "Buffalo" Keaulana, a big wave surfing legend.

Nearly four thousand miles of unobstructed ocean off the coast of Japan end at Oahu's North Shore, producing some of the world's largest waves. When surfers started coming to Hawaii to ride the North Shore's big waves in the 1950s, Buffalo was a lifeguard. It was the golden age of big wave surfing, and Buffalo made his mark on the sport. In a watershed moment for big wave surfing, his longtime partner Greg Noll (after whom Greg Long was named) rode a storied 35-foot wave in 1969, the largest wave anyone had surfed at that time.

Buffalo raised his children in the water and now, in his mideighties, is the patriarch of a big wave surfing dynasty. He stopped surfing only a few years ago. "Surfing is the fountain of youth," his son Brian explains.

In the late 1980s, Brian Keaulana was a contestant in one of the largest big wave surfing competitions, the Eddie (named after the surfer Eddie Aikau), on Waimea Bay. He wiped out in rough water. As Keaulana swam, he thought about a surfer who had recently wiped out and drowned while he was the lifeguard on duty. He couldn't get to the surfer in time because of the turbulent ocean. Now Keaulana found himself in similar conditions, and as he rode out the rough surf, his friend Squiddy came by in a stand-up jet ski and asked if he was okay. Squiddy couldn't rescue him in a stand-up ski, but a "light went on" for Keaulana. He realized jet skis would allow him to reach surfers in much rougher conditions, and he could save more people.

On his way home from the Eddie, Keaulana hunted down all the literature he could find on jet skis. Yamaha had recently released the WaveRunner, a sit-down ski that could make rescues in treacherous waters possible. Keaulana took out a loan, bought one, and started experimenting. After some trial and error, he attached a boogie board to the back as an early rescue sled and started using jet skis in rescues.

A few years later, Keaulana and another lifeguard used jet skis to save seven surfers swept out to sea. When Keaulana returned to the beach, he got a ticket for improper use of a jet ski, which was licensed only for recreation at the time. Keaulana successfully fought the ticket and started lobbying local politicians to change the law, explaining how jet skis could make ocean rescues safer.

The law was changed, and Keaulana helped set up standards and training for using jet skis in water rescues. Today it's normal to see a jet ski parked in the water when surfers tackle big waves. Keaulana smiles as he remembers the first time he brought a jet ski to a major surfing competition. The surfers even stopped the contest while Keaulana ate lunch because they wouldn't surf unless he was nearby on his jet ski.

Soon after Keaulana introduced jet skis, big wave surfers like the legendary Laird Hamilton started using them to take the sport to new heights. Surfers constantly crave big waves, but there used to be limits on the size of waves they could ride because it was too difficult to paddle fast enough to catch very large ones. Hamilton and his friends started using jet skis to launch themselves onto big waves no human could reach by paddling. Called tow-in surfing, this technique makes it possible to ride 70- or 80-foot waves.

Keaulana has done some tow-in surfing himself and doesn't seem bothered by how jet skis have changed the sport. But he worries that people are using them as a crutch to surf waves beyond their skill level: "It gets abused. Maybe people should be out there in ten-foot water, not twenty. They are counting on jet skis to save them and are out there for the wrong reasons—to get noticed, for practice. They count on skis and lifeguards to rescue them. One guy [in large surf] says to me, 'Keep an eye on me, I am not that good.'"

In 1975, the University of Chicago economist Sam Peltzman observed that improving car safety caused more accidents because people took more risks when driving. With power steering, antilock brakes, widespread use of seat belts, and driver-assist alerts if we are too close to another vehicle or pedestrian, cars are safer than ever, but we also drive faster. Taking a bigger risk because technology imparts a feeling of safety is known as the Peltzman effect.

We often fear technology because it means change, but the real downside it poses is that we end up taking even bigger risks because it makes us feel safer.

The challenge facing surfers, financiers, and the rest of us is how to avoid the Peltzman effect and use technology in a less risky way, even as it offers the promise of more thrilling opportunities.

80-FOOT WAVES IN FINANCE

Jet skis in big wave surfing serve the same purpose stock options do in financial markets. Both act as a way to insure against downside risk and still leave unlimited upside. Both can be used to assume even bigger risks, taking on more leverage to amplify returns or surf 80-foot waves. And these big risks pose costs to others. Excessive risk taking in finance spreads risk around and then sometimes requires government bailouts. When surfers need to be rescued, resources are diverted from helping others in need, the lives of rescuers are put at risk, and there is extra expense if the Coast Guard must be called in to assist.

Safety innovations enable people, whether novices or experts, to take on more risk. Sometimes, even for those with the best training and years of experience, that risk goes horribly wrong. Malik Joyeux, Sion Milosky, and Kirk Passmore are among the accomplished big wave surfers who have died within the past two decades.

Robert C. Merton and Myron Scholes, whose formula facilitated the growth of the options market, were partners at Long-Term Capital Management (LTCM), a hedge fund that took on too much risk and nearly caused a financial crisis. The fund, founded in 1994, had the best collection of industry and academic stars on the market. Its primary strategy was to profit off small differences in prices between two bonds with almost the same maturity. The profits from the small differences were tiny, so the fund took on lots of leverage (negative hedge) to amplify risk and the expected return. The risk initially paid off and brought consistently high returns, 40 percent, net of fees, in 1995 and 1996 and slightly less than 20 percent in 1997.

At the end of 1997, the partners decided (after much debate) to return approximately $2.7 billion in capital to LTCM's investors. The firm was more leveraged after the money was returned, which increased not only the potential for bigger profits for the partners but also the risk of insolvency if something went wrong. By the start of 1998, LTCM had about $4.8 billion in equity capital and had borrowed over $124.5 billion, a 25-to-1 leverage ratio.* Returning the money turned out to be the wrong decision.

A few months later Russia devalued its currency and defaulted on its debt. This was followed in short order by the Asian financial crisis. LTCM used risk tools—diversification, hedging, and insurance—to reduce the risk associated with its leverage, but the fund quickly discovered the tools' limitations. Assets that were supposed to offer a hedge suddenly did not. The small price differences between the bonds got much bigger.

LTCM lost money in 1998: within eight months $4.8 billion dwindled to only $2.3 billion. At this rate LTCM couldn't pay back the money it

---

* Leverage ratio is the ratio of debt to equity financing. For equity holders, the bigger the ratio, the greater the risk, because they get a share of the profits: a big payout when the fund does well, and nothing if it tanks. Bondholders have to be paid no matter what.

owed to get all that leverage. The fund also needed money to keep operating, but no one would lend it to them.

The damage from a situation like the one LTCM faced would usually be limited to the investors and partners in the fund. But the risk in this case went beyond LTCM. A large part of its business consisted of acting as an intermediary between different banks that wanted bonds with different maturities. LTCM was a very large player in the market, so most of the large banks would be stuck with bonds they did not want and could not sell if LTCM defaulted.

The Federal Reserve Bank of New York brokered a deal, and fourteen financial firms pooled $3.6 billion for a 90 percent stake in LTCM. This capital injection stopped the bleeding: debts were repaid, markets calmed down, and eventually LTCM was unwound. In the end, the partners and their few remaining investors lost all the money they had put in and earned at the fund. The banks who bought the 90 percent equity share made money and the market remained stable. It was a near miss.

What went on at LTCM has often been held up as a failure of complex risk models. But what went wrong was much simpler. Basically, the fund took on too much risk seeking higher returns. Risk models can't account for everything that can possibly happen, and they are not meant to. A 25-to-1 leverage ratio is the equivalent of surfing an 80-foot wave. You can do all your research, bring jet skis, and wear an inflatable vest, but oceans and financial markets aren't always predictable. There is no way to make an 80-foot wave safe and there is no way to a make a 25-to-1 leverage ratio risk-free.

THE GOLDEN AGE WASN'T SO GOLDEN

It wasn't always so complicated. In the 1950s and '60s, investors in financial markets were more limited to the few people who could afford to lose money, and millions of complicated derivatives weren't used to hedge risk. In Buffalo Keaulana's youth, there were only a few dozen big wave surfers, and they didn't even have a leash to tether them to their long boards (this important safety innovation was introduced in the 1970s). Before surf leashes and jet skis, when surfers wiped out and lost their boards, they might have to swim more than a dozen miles to find a safe place to go ashore. In that era, big wave surfers were all exceptional swimmers and knowledgeable about the ocean. Today almost all surfers have a leash on their boards. When leashes were first introduced, they made surfing more accessible to weaker swimmers. From the moment they were introduced, leashes were controversial and divisive in the surfing community because having them meant less-skilled surfers in the water.

Melvin "Uncle Mel" Pu'u is another surfer at the forefront of risk technology. A large, round, bald man who is father to eight children, he was orphaned at a young age and taken in by the Keaulana family. Uncle Mel and Brian Keaulana grew up as brothers, surfing and lifeguarding, and are so close they finish each other's sentences.

Uncle Mel, Keaulana, and I took a break from the Big Wave Safety Summit and had a lively discussion about the Peltzman effect, or what they call the "double-edged sword of safety." I asked if surfing would be better without all the technology, if we could go back to a simpler time when only surfers with excellent training and superhuman swimming skills like Buffalo were in the water. No waterproof Apple Watches, jet skis, inflatable vests, or surfers who don't belong. "My answer would be no," Uncle Mel said.

> We'd have more deaths. The surfing industry has grown to a level and scale not seen in the early 1950s. Now there's so much exposure and there's more opportunity. When you have this opportunity and equipment, you are going to have people pushing the limits—it just comes with a double-edged sword. There will be those who shouldn't be out there, taking advantage of the technology at hand. . . . It

becomes an issue of maybe it would be better if we didn't [have all the safety tools], but it becomes a necessity that we do.

"It also helped us understand our mind and our physical limits," Keaulana added.

Because we could never test our limits without the use of technology. No one surfed North Shore before. Mostly military people came here, they died, then [we got] better boards [and thought], oh we can surf this. Then the jet ski came and we went to the outer reefs. It raised the level of what our minds and bodies can do out in the environment with proper use of technology, but it takes the right people with the right equipment.

I had asked them this question about surfing's golden age, but people often ask the same question about financial markets. The logic goes that the world would be better off if the financial derivatives that came from Black-Scholes disappeared and we returned to smaller, simpler financial markets. When I brought up this parallel to Uncle Mel and Keaulana, the first question they asked me was "Aren't those [financial derivatives] used to cheat people?" But just as jet skis and inflatable vests offer safety to surfers who want to pursue bigger waves, the intent of most financial innovation is to find ways to offer investors security while they still enjoy some upside from taking risk.

In both surfing and finance, better insurance means more opportunity and growth. Financial innovation promises to offer cheaper and less-risky ways to finance new technology. As technology evolves, so does the financial tools that finances it. New innovations in finance that made it possible to manage risk can explain everything from the rise of Ancient Rome to the growth of modern cities. The evolution of finance since the 1970s powered more risk taking, which has meant more wealth flowing to poor countries, more development, and less global poverty. In richer countries, financial innovation has made advances we enjoy to-day possible. A more global, integrated economy requires financial tools that did not exist in the 1950s and '60s.

Sometimes risks don't work out, but this is the price we pay for a growing economy and more prosperity. The trick is finding ways that limit the collateral damage from risks gone wrong.

HOW CAN WE DO BETTER?

Safety innovation may mean more risk taking, but overall we are safer and richer. The number of deaths in traffic accidents has fallen since the 1970s, even though we drive more miles. However, starting in 2016 the trend reversed, and there was a small uptick in fatal accidents. One reason for the increase is mobile phones. They make us safer because we can call for help if something goes wrong, but they also make driving more dangerous if you text while behind the wheel.

With derivatives, more people invest, which means more wealth. Investment flows more readily to parts of the economy it did not before, which means more small businesses and developing countries get capital. But sometimes the risks don't pay off and everyone suffers, even if we are better off overall.

The fact that any risk innovation empowers us to take more risk is exactly why regularly updating regulations is necessary, whether in financial markets, the auto industry, or surfing. What Brian Keaulana did should be a model of how we, and regulators especially, should approach safety innovations. First he changed the rules for jet skis when he discovered they were a useful safety device. Then he focused on education so people use the tools responsibly. Now the state of Hawaii requires certification to use jet skis for tow-in surfing.

Most of us aren't lucky enough to know someone like Keaulana who provides the intellectual leadership his industry needs. Regulations like speed limits on highways and capital ratios for banks can curb some of our worst impulses to take on more risk. But as long as we constantly innovate new ways to reduce risk and thereby create an opportunity to take more risks regulation will constantly struggle to keep pace with the latest innovation.

It ultimately falls on us to be mindful of the risks we take. Risk offers the possibility of more, and risk management tools aim to empower us to go for more while taking less risk. Using them correctly involves staying focused on our goals and taking just enough risk to achieve them. Keaulana and BWRAG aim to make surfers more thoughtful about risk so they don't take more risk than they need to and still enjoy the upside of surfing the large swells.

The modern world offers you the chance to take bigger risks than you should, like surfing a 50-foot wave when you barely know how to swim or using a financial derivative to take on tons of leverage to bet on a stock. Each of these options offers the chance for huge rewards, but it is worth asking if that reward is really your goal, and if it is worth swimming in shark-filled waters to get it.

RULE 5

UNCERTAINTY HAPPENS

"Man plans and God laughs" is a Yiddish proverb. The same can be said for managing risk. Risk is everything you can imagine happening in the future. Risk management takes control of the risk we anticipate. But sometimes something goes wrong (or right) you never could have imagined or planned for.

Even the best risk strategies and most accurate risk estimates can't account for everything. We might make calculated choices based on data-based probability measures; it's the best we can do most of the time and helps us reduce risk 90 percent of the time. But how do we deal with the other 10 percent, or the Knightian uncertainty, which is the risk we can't predict,* or what the former defense secretary Donald Rumsfeld called "unknown unknowns"?

Chapter 12 explains how to prepare for uncertainty. Some people are skeptical of risk management because it only protects us from the risks we can plan for and lulls us into safety. But it is possible to plan for the unplannable. It often comes down to managing the risk you can imagine and retaining just the right amount of flexibility for the unexpected.

---

* The economist Frank Knight first differentiated between risk, the possibilities you can measure, and uncertainty, the unpredictable, in 1921. This kind of uncertainty is sometimes called Knightian uncertainty in his honor.

UNCERTAINTY:
The Fog of War

Plans are worthless, but planning is everything.

—DWIGHT D. EISENHOWER

Arguably, no institution puts more resources into risk management than the military. They also pay the biggest cost if their plans fall short, and they inevitably do. When it comes to warfare, everything is uncertain and things rarely go as planned.

No one can predict how a risky decision will turn out, even when the stakes are much lower. Risk measurement is our best guess of what will happen, and risk management stacks the odds in your favor. But this all assumes our estimate of risk is a good one; we can anticipate most of the risky possibilities. But what about the remaining uncertainty, the things we never saw coming? How can we plan for the unimaginable?

The retired general H. R. McMaster is legendary in military circles for his decisive battle victories. He is more widely known for his tumultuous year in the White House as President Trump's second national security adviser. But what many people don't know is that he is also one of the foremost experts on risk in warfare and how to plan for the unpredictable.

THE BATTLE OF 73 EASTING

On February 23, 1991, Eagle Troop of the Second Squadron, Second Armored Cavalry Regiment, crossed the Saudi-Iraqi border. It was the start of the ground campaign of Operation Desert Storm, and the regiment's mission was to envelop and defeat the Iraqi Republican Guard from the west.

Eagle Troop was led by Captain H. R. McMaster, then a twenty-eight-year-old West Point graduate. He commanded Eagle Troop's 140 soldiers, who were organized into two tank platoons. Spirits were high among the soldiers; most had never seen combat and were exhilarated to be behind enemy lines. It had been a generation since a major U.S. combat operation. The soldiers were trained for this, but they never expected they would actually go into battle.

The Gulf War was the first American war since Vietnam. Like all wars, the highest ranks of the military went through careful risk planning. The Pentagon ran simulations that tried to anticipate all the things that might happen. They determined which tactics and equipment would minimize the worst possible outcome. The military prepared for the worst; they anticipated that removing Saddam Hussein from Kuwait would cost tens of thousands of American soldiers' lives. To a certain extent, these predictions were based on the Vietnam War, in addition to intelligence on how well armed and trained the Iraqi forces were assumed to be.

Eagle Troop was both tense and excited. They expected a tough enemy, but in the first few days after crossing the border, McMaster and his troops were surprised to hear stories about how easily other troops in the regiment had dominated the Iraqi soldiers.

On the evening of the twenty-fourth, an Eagle Troop scout spotted Iraqi soldiers. McMaster fired his tank, killing some Iraqis; some ran off, and several others surrendered. It was the first time Eagle Troop experienced enemy contact and it went quickly and easily. It was not what they expected. McMaster warned the soldiers not to get too complacent. The troop still had not encountered the Republican Guard, the elite offensive unit in the Iraqi army.

Over the next few days, Eagle Troop moved farther into Iraq. For the first time, the soldiers saw dead Iraqis killed by allied troops. They also encountered Iraqi soldiers who'd thrown down their weapons, some of whom greeted Eagle Troop cheerfully with thumbs-up signs, appearing to even cheer on the U.S. troops. McMaster described them in desperate need of food and water: "They were ragged, wearied, mustachioed, dark-haired men with nothing but their solid green uniforms and boots."

On the morning of the twenty-sixth, Eagle Troop awoke to a heavy fog that eventually cleared and was replaced by a sandstorm. The storm grounded the air cavalry, which meant the troop lacked the insurance of air support if they were injured in battle and had to be evacuated for medical assistance.

Before 10:00 a.m., Eagle Troop spotted three Iraqi tanks on a scouting mission. Another troop from the regiment had already destroyed two of the tanks, so it was now McMaster's turn to take care of the third. He called in on his radio, "Does that MTLB [the Iraqi tank] have my name on it?" The response was "Roger, your name's written all over it."

The tank was 2,000 meters away. McMaster's tank computer made calculations based on the wind and speed of the target. He waited for the right moment and yelled, "Fire!"

The Iraqi tank burst into flames as the sound of the cannon's boom reverberated through the cabin of McMaster's tank and filled it with the smell of gunpowder. His soldiers chided him for not allowing them to fire on the Iraqi tank—everyone wanted in on the action. Eagle Troop was feeling frustrated and anxious by the frequent starts and stops. They had never fought even a small battle before and soon might be facing the Republican Guard. Once they were under heavy fire, a moment's hesitation could cost them their lives.

They pressed forward, tasked with gaining more ground, and by noon had reached 60 easting. (Easting is a measure, in meters, of distance [eastward]). By 3:25, they received orders to advance to 70 easting but no farther. While they knew the general location of their target, Eagle Troop did not have detailed intelligence on what they'd face. McMaster had a feeling they were approaching the enemy; he told his troops, "This is the moment we have all awaited."

The sandstorm meant poor visibility, and because they had no maps, Eagle Troop pushed through the desert, unaware a road ran parallel to them. They also did not know they were entering the training ground of the elite Tawakalna Division of the Republican Guard, who had been tasked with halting their entry into Kuwait.

The enemy commander, Major Mohammed (who had trained at Fort Benning, Georgia, when Iraq and the United States were allies), planned to defend his position from the village the road bisected. He was unaware that the Americans had navigation equipment that allowed Eagle Troop to transverse the desert instead of having to stay on the road. The technology was new: the Gulf War was the first GPS war; it freed Eagle Troop from relying on traditional maps and roads. Major Mohammed fortified his defensive position along the road and prepared to take the army out as it entered the village. Hundreds of Iraqi soldiers in bunkers awaited the 140-person Eagle Troop.

But Eagle Troop, approaching from the desert instead of the road, bypassed the village, surprised the Iraqi troops, fired on them, and pressed on with the tanks leading in a V formation.

By 4:18 p.m., the sandstorm still raged on as the tank platoon crested a steep rise in the desert, only to be met by a large element of the Iraqi Republican Guard. For the first time since they had entered enemy territory, Eagle Troop came under intense fire. Twenty-three minutes of the most dramatic and decisive battle of the Gulf War followed.

Well-practiced but inexperienced in combat, Eagle Troop did not break stride, firing back quickly and prevailing over their enemy. Mc-Master recalled, "I remember feeling proud of how the Troop reacted. Falling artillery [being under fire] is something difficult to replicate in training but the troopers reacted exactly as we had practiced."

Practice and training were certainly critical, but Eagle Troop also got lucky. The sandstorm meant no one had good visibility, but Eagle Troop had better technology, so they could still find and then surprise the Iraqi defenses.

Eagle Troop pressed eastward, encountering more Iraqi soldiers. The enemy defense was more formidable than the last, with thirty tanks, fourteen other armored vehicles, and several hundred infantry, a much bigger force than Eagle Troop. But Eagle Troop's superior training, better equipment, and the element of surprise more than compensated for its smaller numbers and unfamiliarity with the terrain.

The fighting went quickly. Eagle Troop destroyed dozens of Iraqi tanks within several minutes and was set to keep moving east. That's when a lieutenant from command radioed McMaster that he had already gone too far, reminding him he wasn't supposed to cross 70 easting. McMaster said, "Tell them I'm sorry," and continued on.

Reflecting on this decision more than twenty-five years later, McMaster still thinks he made the right choice. Once they pushed beyond 70 easting, they surprised and defeated another Iraqi reserve force that was in the process of organizing for battle. If they had stopped 3 kilometers back as instructed, the Iraqis could have reorganized and launched a successful counterattack. McMaster explained his decision in a detailed account of the battle:

> If we had stopped, we would have forfeited the shock effect we inflicted on the enemy. Had we halted, we would have given the enemy farther to the east an opportunity to organize an effort against us while we presented them with stationary targets. We had the

advantage and had to finish the battle rapidly. We would press the attack until all of the enemy were destroyed or until they surrendered.

They pressed on to further victory. Shortly after 4:40, they finally stopped, a little shy of 74 easting, where the fighting ceased.

Eagle Troop suffered no casualties* and defeated an entire battalion of Iraq's best soldiers, a much larger force with more than ten times the number of tanks. This battle, particularly those critical twenty-three minutes, became known as the Battle of 73 Easting, one of the most decisive victories in the Gulf War.

Despite his snap judgment and stunning victory, not everyone was pleased with McMaster. Going a few kilometers farther in the heat of battle might not sound like a big deal, but in the military, following orders to the letter is important. McMaster told me he was reprimanded by his superiors because he "risked the lives of soldiers in a wanton manner." The decision may have made him a hero to some, but it and other decisions like it throughout his career may have slowed his advancement through the military ranks. While McMaster was very successful and eventually became a three-star general, his outspoken nature may have kept him from a coveted fourth star.

Battles like the one fought at 73 easting changed how the Pentagon thought about war. To many in the top brass, it demonstrated that the United States had the strongest, best-equipped military in the world. In the years following the Gulf War, a dominant school of thought emerged: it assumed that America's superior technology could remove risk from warfare. In the mid-1990s, Admiral William Owens, the vice chairman of the Joint Chiefs of Staff, said, on several occasions, that technology could enable U.S. military forces in the future to lift the "fog of war." McMaster recalled people at the Pentagon saying the

---

* The Second Squadron's Ghost Troop suffered one casualty.

American military was so strong, no country would dare challenge it. McMaster told me he'd even heard the top brass use a market analogy: "They'd say we priced other armies out of the market."

Thanks to new technology and the end of the Cold War, the military figured it could get by with a leaner force and centralize power within the highest levels of command. Consequently, the United States shrank the size of its military.

Given his leadership in this notable battle, one that influenced U.S. military strategy for the next decade, what McMaster did after the Gulf War is all the more remarkable. While still on active duty, he went to the University of North Carolina at Chapel Hill to earn a PhD in history; he wrote his dissertation on the Vietnam War. He focused on the civilians who worked at the Pentagon who had pushed for the United States to go to war with Vietnam based on data and risk models that failed to account for the political and social complexity that existed there. Meanwhile, military generals feared speaking out about the reality of what was happening on the ground. McMaster later published his dissertation as a successful book, fittingly called *Dereliction of Duty: Lyndon Johnson, Robert McNamara, the Joint Chiefs of Staff, and the Lies That Led to Vietnam.*

UNKNOWN UNKNOWNS

While most of us will never experience combat in our lifetime, we can still learn from McMaster's experience on the battlefield and better prepare for what we don't see coming. We usually face safer, lower-stakes interactions, though often still emotional and unpredictable: negotiating with your family about who to spend the holidays with, asking your boss for a raise, or having to fight for a lucrative client against a toxic colleague. In any of these situations, getting what we want—a joyful holiday, a raise, that client—requires taking a risk in an emotionally charged situation in which our rational, thoughtful risk planning can't perfectly predict how things play out.

When we face these interactions, even the best risk management strategy can fall short because the world and how people behave is inherently uncertain. Risk models are valuable, but they can backfire if you assume the unpredictable has become completely predictable. Suppose you decide to take a risk and demand a raise from your boss. If you operate under the assumption you are invaluable, you might threaten to quit. You might be invaluable, but if you go in unaware of some top secret information, like the company is facing financial trouble and planning lay-offs, or if your boss is just having a bad day, you may find yourself out of a job because you didn't anticipate this in your risk calculation.

And yet the fact that our estimates aren't perfect doesn't justify giving up on risk management altogether. Using risk tools well requires being mindful of their limitations. If the tools work 90 percent or even 10 percent of the time, it is better than doing nothing (though we aim for the higher end rather than the lower). Learning how to measure and manage risk was one of the great advances of the Renaissance and Enlightenment periods, freeing humans from superstition and paving the way for many of the improvements we enjoy today. So instead of shunning risk management, let's figure out how best to use it, while acknowledging uncertainty—and learning from a master about how to deal with it better.

McMaster has spent his career writing about and dealing with warfare's most unpredictable elements. He looks like a younger, shorter version of the Moonlite BunnyRanch's Dennis Hof and speaks quickly in a hoarse, booming voice. Outspoken and fiercely intellectual, he has often stood out, for good and bad, in the rigid military structure. He has the sharp mind of a history professor trapped in the body of an imposing general. Conversations with him are peppered with quotes from Greek philosophers and many book recommendations. Just like a professor, he gave me reading assignments and instructions to get back to him with notes.

We spoke mere weeks before he was named the national security adviser to President Trump. At that time, he was at a crossroads, planning on leaving the military after a lifetime of service. He ultimately decided to serve his country for another year in the Trump administration and stay in the military during his time. He calls his year in the White House the "bonus year" of his storied military career.

Compared with leading people into combat, it was a very different kind of risk. Weeks before taking it on, he explained the hazards of risk planning in war to me. He said, "If you try to plan for everything and think you have too much certainty, you create vulnerabilities. If you try too hard to predict everything that can happen and shift from the realm of certainty to uncertainty, you are going to build vulnerabilities into your force."

This insight is a good rule of thumb for dealing with risks not just in the military—where the limitations of risk management are apparent—but in everyday life. When we are leaving a job we are comfortable with, moving to a new city, or taking on any new challenge, we can never anticipate everything that will go wrong or right, and if we think we can, we set ourselves up for failure.

No institution spends more time and energy on risk planning than the military. They use models and techniques to figure out how to reduce risk at every level for war—the equipment they need, the number of troops, and what to target. The field of engineering known as operations research was developed specifically for the military. It takes a similar approach to risk as finance by first defining an objective and then finding the best way to achieve it while minimizing downside risk.

All this planning is meant to reduce risk, but war, even with lots of risk-reducing technology, will always be unpredictable. The one thing you can count on is that the unexpected will happen. The Prussian general and philosopher of war Carl von Clausewitz identified several factors that make war inherently uncertain and impossible to predict: the "politics" of war, the human dimension of war, the complexity of war, and the interaction or nonlinearity of war.

You might try to plan for every way a battle can go and have better technology that gives you a huge advantage, but war is a contest of wills, and it is impossible to know how your enemy will respond.

Sometimes the military encounters a stronger, more resilient enemy than they planned for; other times a freak sandstorm gives them an advantage they need to capitalize on. How to plan well enough so soldiers go in prepared and still retain sufficient flexibility to handle in-the-moment battle decisions is a tension faced by the armed forces of all nations. How they strike that balance explains many of their successes and failures on the battlefield.

DOOMED TO REPEAT HISTORY BECAUSE WE ARE OFTEN BLIND TO UNCERTAINTY

Risk planning can lull us into a false comfort that we have fully prepared for anything that might happen. It is a seductive narrative because we want to believe that the future is under our control. The first step in dealing with uncertainty is coming to terms with the fact that, no matter how much we plan, pore over data, and insure ourselves, we still face some uncertainty. We can reduce uncertainty but never eliminate it. This is a hard lesson to accept, one that has doomed many military campaigns.

It could be argued that the military fights the previous war—that planning for the Iraq War was based on what happened in the Gulf War, and planning for the Gulf War was based on what happened in Vietnam. But that is an oversimplification; according to the historian Williamson Murray, military organizations learn the lessons they want to learn:

"The fact is that military organizations, for the most part, study what makes them feel comfortable about themselves, not the uncongenial lessons of past conflicts. The result is that more often than not, militaries have to relearn in combat—and usually at a heavy cost lessons that were readily apparent at the end of the last conflict."

We can see this in the aftermath of the Gulf War. It sparked the Revolution in Military Affairs, a philosophy that the latest technology was so powerful it could reduce, or even eliminate, much of the risk in warfare. The Revolution in Military Affairs permeated the Pentagon; it justified shrinking the military into a smaller, lighter, more efficient organization. Future wars were planned based on the assumption that technology could make war fast and cheap, without incurring many American casualties.

But this was only one possible lesson from the Gulf War, albeit a compelling one. War is horrible, the worst thing humans do. People die terrible deaths and sometimes nothing is resolved in spite of their sacrifice. War is also unpredictable, and taking risks is the only way to win. It is natural to fall for the idea that you can get all the benefits of war— global hegemony or fortune—and reduce the terrible costs. But it was the wrong lesson. The right one is that you can't predict your enemy. It would have been better to study the small decisions made by officers like McMaster, who knew how to deal with surprises on the battlefield.

History is full of empires falling after making this mistake. Following World War I, French military doctrine and institutional culture developed in a way similar to that of U.S. armed forces after the Gulf War. The French convinced themselves that new technology—tanks and planes—could reduce the risk of warfare, and they centralized command at the highest levels.

The Israeli colonel Meir Finkel argues that France's downfall in World War II resulted from their creating a rigidity in how they approached battle. Troop movements were practically fully choreographed in advance on the assumption that battles had become more predictable. Hitler observed this and instructed his generals "to operate and to act quickly, something that does not come easily to the systematic French or to the ponderous English."

Unlike the French forces, who went into battle with rigid top-down commands, the Germans were trained to improvise and maneuver. The French were shocked by the more agile, fast-moving German enemy. The Germans took over France in just a few weeks.

McMaster calls this belief that technology can eliminate risk in warfare and make it fast and cheap the "vampire fallacy," because it just won't die. It is easy to see why the military, or any of us, would be seduced by the idea that we can eliminate uncertainty. Uncertainty makes us uncomfortable, and it is costly to deal with.

McMaster says it is a sign of overconfidence in certainty when the military centralizes power at the highest levels of command. This is how we'd like to fight wars; it is relatively cheap and easy. Accepting and preparing for uncertainty is harder and more expensive. It requires having many well-trained troops empowered to make decisions on the ground in the way that McMaster took it upon himself at 73 easting.

It may sound chaotic, even risky, to train soldiers to change plans and modify orders on the fly. But if they are well trained, they know when it is necessary to do this and how. McMaster says practice, education, and training are critical. He has his troops go through battle drills and learn the culture and language of the country they are fighting in. Practice gives them confidence to make the right decision and not hesitate when something they don't expect happens. Even if things don't go according to plan, the training and learning how to work as a team keep soldiers rational in the most stressful circumstances imaginable. Training and tackling various battlefield simulations also enable soldiers to think creatively and be open to things unfolding in ways different from what they expect.

But a large, well-trained military is expensive to produce and maintain. Preparing for uncertainty requires the flexibility McMaster describes, and just like traditional risk management, flexibility comes at a cost.

HOW TO DEAL WITH UNCERTAINTY

Using risk measurement and management when you make a decision, big or small, is similar to taking a road trip with a map. The map certainly increases the odds of a successful journey, but it can't tell you if a truck will smash into your car. You still need to be an alert driver and swerve out of the way of an oncoming truck.

In warfare this means flexibility, or well-prepared troops who are empowered to make decisions on the fly. As Colonel Finkel writes in his book *On Flexibility: Recovery from Technological and Doctrinal Surprise on the Battlefield,* "The solution to . . . surprise lies not in predicting the nature of the future battlefield or obtaining information about the enemy's preparations for the coming war, *but in the ability to recuperate swiftly from the initial surprise.*"

To be able to handle the unexpected, an army must develop four elements, Finkel argues, that can help them retain the flexibility they need to react to the unanticipated. The principles work both in warfare and in daily life:

1. Create an atmosphere that encourages lower-ranking commanders to come up with new ideas that challenge the official doctrine—and be heard. Soldiers must feel able to voice their own ideas, even if it goes against the conventional wisdom and prevailing strategy. This facilitates a balanced view of a conflict and avoids "getting too stuck in a dogmatic rut."
2. Realize that "super weapons," no matter how impressive, "eventually will be confronted with [effective] countermeasures." Then the military will need other technology.

3. Have a system that encourages "fast learning and rapid circulation of lessons" learned. This requires sharing information quickly and interpreting it correctly.

4. Employ commanders who have the mental flexibility to change strategy when circumstances change. This requires "an environment that encourages questioning and creativity" and offers excellent training. It is a hard balance—the military wants soldiers to have some autonomy, but advanced planning and organization are also critical. That is why it is so important to have well-trained troops. When things fall apart in battle, it is easy to lose your head and panic, so training and preparation help soldiers stay calm and rational.

We can generalize this advice to many aspects of our lives. In work it can be openness to junior colleagues. Even if you find a certain know-it-all millennial frustrating, there is often a grain of valuable wisdom in his or her opinions. Maintaining flexibility requires us to be open-minded to ideas that make us uncomfortable and to finding solutions in unexpected places. Of course, it takes experience and expertise to tell a good novel idea from a bad one. The more we know the market and the risks that typically do crop up, the easier it is to spot a good idea. The tension is tempering expertise with humility.

Finkel's lessons are also valuable in deciding how we integrate technology into our lives. It is wonderful to be so connected, but hackers and scammers can also use that technology against us. It feels like every time we come up with ways to evade them, and we feel safe, they find another way into our lives. Cyber risk poses a constant source of uncertainty, and it's a risk we can't measure. All we can do is stay flexible and constantly adopt new ways to defend ourselves: installing software security patches as soon as they are available, using two-stage authentication, and changing our passwords regularly.

Most important, we need to retain the option to change course when our plans go awry and have the humility to follow through. Kat Cole, the waitress turned executive, may have dropped out of college to work full-time at Hooters, but she always kept the option of going back to school alive by taking online classes. She says she often takes risks that don't work out: "You can't Bubble Wrap an initiative and anticipate everything that can go wrong." But she retains some flexibility and is willing to recognize when something isn't working and change course quickly. She says this takes humility and being open to other people's opinions.

WHAT WE ALL NEED TO LEARN FROM THE MILITARY

The uncertain nature of war means it will always be risky. Whether or not the risks of a military campaign are worth the human cost is the question that makes or breaks empires. And whether or not they are successful in their endeavors comes not only from good planning but from planning for the unexpected, and this is where they, and all of us, often fall short.

The idea that the latest technology can remove risk from warfare and make what is a fundamentally risky endeavor safe mirrors a similar hubris in financial markets. Before the 2008 crisis, economists spoke about "the Great Moderation," the idea that policy and risk management had removed the risk of financial crises and catastrophic recessions. Some also argued that financial derivatives and hedging strategies like securitized mortgages had removed the risk from markets.

The Great Moderation and the infallibility of risk management turned out to be wrong too. A financial crisis few saw coming nearly caused another Great Depression.

When it comes to finance, just like war, rigidity is where things go wrong. A lack of flexibility is also why leverage, or negative hedging, is so risky. If something happens you don't expect, you may not have any money, but you still need to pay your debt. This is what the big banks and many households did. Taking on more debt is like centralizing power at the highest ranks of the military. It works sometimes, but if things don't turn out the way you expect, you are in trouble.

It is popular to keep score of who saw the crisis coming and who didn't. But this is the wrong approach to uncertainty. No one gets their predictions right all the time. Almost everyone who "called" the financial crisis made several wrong predictions afterward.

Instead we should pay attention to great risk takers, the ones who hedge, insure, and retain some flexibility and resilience, because they have the most to teach us. It may seem they are overly cautious when the market is booming and they don't take big risks, but really, they accept things will happen that they don't anticipate. They create enough flexibility to handle surprises, both good and bad.

They understand that even the best tools, risk planning, and technology can't change the nature of war, financial markets, the course of our careers, or finding our partner. Once human behavior is involved, nothing is ever totally predictable. Risk tools—good planning, data, diversification, hedging, and insurance—give us some certainty, but they can never guarantee that people won't lose money investing in markets, that surfers won't drown, that wars won't be lost, that we won't lose our jobs or experience heartbreak.

McMaster, an outspoken critic on the limitations of risk models, still uses them. He argues the best way to deal with uncertainty is to go into battle prepared and educated. The process of risk measurement and management forces us to think through our objectives, what the risks are, and how we can reduce risk. This process also educates us on what we might expect on the ground.

If you are asking for a raise and take the time to think through what you are willing to accept, what you want from your career, and how much your boss can afford to pay, you'll face fewer surprises. Then create room to be flexible. If you go in only willing to accept a 20 percent increase, you create too much rigidity and a vulnerability if your boss does surprise you. You can also retain some flexibility by offering your boss options, such as different ways to expand your role for more money or more vacation time instead of salary. This flexibility gives you room to pivot and keep your resolve.

Risk measurement and risk management offer the most valuable ways to deal with risk and uncertainty. But like anything else, if they are used incorrectly, they create more risk than they prevent. The key is to use them well but still be prepared to change strategies and be ready for the unexpected.

FINAL THOUGHTS

We must take risks to move our lives forward. Understanding risk and knowing how to take smart risks is a critical life skill, and yet the science of risk is rarely taught. This may explain why we tend to think of risk in a binary way: either you take a risk or you don't; either you have certainty or the future is totally random and unpredictable. It is no wonder that taking a risk feels overwhelming or scary.

The lessons from financial economics in this book offer another alternative, a more realistic and useful approach to risk. It is not a question of either you have certainty or you don't; odds are you never have certainty, but some situations pose more risk than others. The more we embrace the degrees of uncertainty that exist in our lives, the more we can deal with it and thrive.

"How can I take smarter risks?" should be the question instead of "Should I take a risk?" The central lesson from financial economics is that risk is the cost we pay to get more. People who take risks tend to get more, but they face the possibility of loss. We can reduce risk, but that comes at a price.

This all suggests a different approach to risk.

Smart risk takers don't back away from risky situations. Instead of debating whether or not to take a risk, go for what you want: measure the risk involved and then take only as much as you need to in order to get what you want.

Knowing how to take just enough risk increases the odds our risks will work out and we can get more from life. It does not offer any guarantees but can embolden us to take risks more frequently and go for more. In a fast-shifting, technology-driven economy that at once threatens to change our jobs and way of life but also offers the possibility for so much more, we need to understand risk now more than ever.

When I wrote this book, the easiest part was finding great risk takers in places that have nothing to do with traditional finance. People who are successful at what they do, whether it is surfing, stalking celebrities, or going into battle, manage their risk well. We all are smart risk takers in at least one aspect of our lives and have the potential to apply the same reasoning to every decision we make.

We can do this by understanding the science behind risk: how to define risk, how to measure it, how to identify the type of risk we face, and how to manage it. Financial economics is the science of risk, and it provides a structure to help us understand what makes a good risk to take.

Once we know what works and why, we can apply our risk-taking strategy to any decision we make. Even investing for retirement and getting to the airport become easier and less overwhelming.

Use the tools well, take more risks, and be ready for the unexpected.

Acknowledgments

It took an army of kind, generous, and patient people to write this book. First, I must thank Robert C. Merton, who inspired me to write it, helped plot out the structure, and provided helpful comments on the chapters. You reminded me what risk is: whatever is not risk-free.

I am beyond grateful to everyone I interviewed and profiled in this book. Your stories are what made this book possible. You took a risk by letting me tell your life story. I hope I did you justice.

I also had a small army of readers, especially Robin Epstein and Jason Levine, who read multiple drafts of every chapter and offered invaluable feedback. I also got very useful comments from Emily Rueb, Stacey Vanick-Smith, Peter Hancock, Chris Wiggins, Lisa Cowen, Byron Rogers, Kodjo Apedjinou, Praveen Korapaty, Jenna Reinen, Hal Vogel, Ross Fermer, David Pullman, Jill Stowe, Brandon Archuleta, and Peyo Lizarazu.

Most of the topics in this book were new to me. I had the crazy idea that financial economics can explain any market, but first I had to learn about these markets. Often this required infiltrating a whole new, sometimes secretive, subculture. That would not have been possible without the army of experts who were kind enough to spend hours explaining how it all works and introducing me to the right people.

I am grateful to Jeremy Lemur for arranging all my interviews in the Hof brothels, Dennis Hof for giving me free rein in his brothels—I wish you had lived to see this book—and Madam Suzette for encouraging the women to speak with me. A special thanks to Farrah Banks, Cassandra Claire, and Ruby Rae. Thanks to Scott Cunningham for help with the data.

Jon Sloss, Ross Fermer, and David Shaheen and his whole team at JPMorgan made the movie chapter possible. I also must thank Dan Goldstein and Jenna Reinen for explaining to me, an efficient-markets fundamentalist, why behavioral economics is so important. And a big thank-you to Mike Naft and Osi Gerald for sharing your stories and introducing me to everyone at the Fortune Society.

I am grateful to all the people in Kentucky who gave me so much of their time and explained the secrets of their industry to me: Frank Mitchell, Emmeline Hill (in Ireland), Grant Williamson, Bernie Sams, David Lambert, and Ed DeRosa.

A huge thank-you to the person at Carnival who transcribed my two-and-a-half-hour interview with Arnold Donald. I don't know your name, but I am eternally grateful.

I am grateful to Mark Healey and everyone at BWRAG, especially Ian Masterson and Liam Wilmot, who were so welcoming. I owe a debt of gratitude to Chris Gough; when I cold-called you and said I was writing a book about finance and wanted to interview surfers, you did not miss a beat and said, "You made the right call." At that moment I knew this chapter would work.

Thanks to Max Boot for introducing me to General H. R. McMaster and to Kevin Kawasaki for explaining how the army manages risk.

A big thank-you to Kevin Delany, Lauren Brown, Jason Karaian, and Kabir Chibir at Quartz. Kevin, you took a risk and believed in me. You gave me the opportunity and platform to explore Quartzy markets, which made it possible to develop as a writer and as an economist. I needed that to pull this off.

ACKNOWLEDGMENTS

A huge thank-you to my editor, Stephanie Frerich, and everyone at Portfolio, especially Bria and Rebecca, who immediately got this book and loved it as much as I do. Your edits made this book everything it is. Maureen Clark, your copy edits were phenomenal; thank you for taking such care and attention, and making me sound like a much better writer. Another big thanks to my agent, Mel Flashman, who made this process so much fun.

And a big thanks and an apology to anyone I missed; I am sure there are many of you.

And finally, I owe everything to my wonderful, supportive family—my mother, my father, Steve, Terry, Josh, Staci, and Dakota. You never questioned any of my life choices. You held my hand through every minute of graduate school. You remained unwavering in your support, even when I did some very strange things with my degree. You made it possible for me to feel safe enough to take risks.

Notes

CHAPTER 1: INTRODUCING RISK

2 **sex-worker homicides:** D. D. Brewer et al., "Extent, Trends, and Perpetrators of Prostitution-Related Homicide in the United States," *Journal of Forensic Sciences* 51, no. 5 (September 2006): 1101–8.

3 **"hope for economic success":** Rolf Skjong, "Etymology of Risk: Classical Greek Origin—Nautical Expression—Metaphor for 'Difficulty to Avoid in the Sea,'" February 25, 2005, http://research.dnv.com/skj/Papers/ETYMOLOGY-OF-RISK.pdf.

9 **sex using four years' worth:** Data was scraped from the Internet by a researcher who wishes to remain anonymous and was kind enough to share it with me.

9 **prostitutes who work with pimps:** Steven Levitt and Sudhir Venkatesh, "An Empirical Analysis of Street-Level Prostitution," unpublished manuscript, 2007, http://international.ucla.edu/institute/article/85677.

10 **Economists have estimated:** Paul Gertier, Manisha Shah, and Stefano M. Bertozzi, "Risky Business: The Market for Unprotected Commercial Sex," *Journal of Political Economy* 113, no. 3 (June 2005): 518–50.

17 **estimated) and uncertainty:** Frank Knight, *Risk, Uncertainty, and Profit* (Boston: Houghton Mifflin Co., 1921).

CHAPTER 2: REWARD

26 **lower-calorie alternative:** From interviews with Cole in 2016 and 2017.

CHAPTER 4: RISK MEASUREMENT

46 **elaborate Excel spreadsheet:** Chris Jones, "Ryan Kavanaugh Uses Math to Make Movies," *Esquire,* November 19, 2009. https://www.esquire.com/news-politics/a6641/ryan-kavanaugh-1209/.

49 **"making this investment":** Connie Bruck, "Cashier du Cinema," *New Yorker*, October 8, 2012, https://www.newyorker.com/magazine/2012/10/08/cashier-du-cinema.

50 **couldn't be measured:** Peter Bernstein, *Against the Gods: The Remarkable Story of Risk* (Hoboken, NJ: John Wiley & Sons, 1996).

53 **conforming to this shape:** Eugene Fama, "The Behavior of Stock-Market Prices," *Journal of Business* 38, no. 1 (January 1965): 34–105.

54 **all movies released:** Data from Nash Information Services, http://nashinfoservices.com/.

55 **the exact same shape:** Arthur De Vany and W. David Walls, "Uncertainty in the Movie Industry: Does Star Power Reduce the Terror of the Box Office?," *Journal of Cultural Economics* 23, no. 4 (November 1999): 285–318.

57 **average horror movie:** Estimated from data from Nash Information Services.

58 **"Holy Grail" of Hollywood:** Alex Ben Block, "Ryan Kavanaugh's Secret to Success," *Hollywood Reporter,* September 29, 2010, https://www.hollywoodreporter.com/news/ryan-kavanaughs-secret-success-28540.

58 **between 13 percent and 18 percent:** Tatiana Siegal, "Gun Hill Slate a Sound Investment,"

Variety, October 14, 2007, https://variety.com/2007/film/markets-festivals/gun-hill-slate-a-sound-investment-1117974039/.

59 **U.S. earnings of only $539,000:** Benjamin Wallace, "The Epic Fail of Hollywood's Hottest Algorithm," *New York Magazine,* January 25, 2016, http://www.vulture.com/2016/01/relativity-media-ryan-kavanaugh-c-v-r.html.

60 **reporter Ben Fritz:** Ben Fritz, *The Big Picture: The Fight for the Future of Movies* (New York: Houghton Mifflin, 2018).

60 **executive David Shaheen:** From interviews with Shaheen and his team at JP Morgan.

CHAPTER 5: DIFFERENT TYPES OF RISK

73 **economists William Sharpe and John Lintner:** William F. Sharpe, "Capital Asset Prices: A Theory of Market Equilibrium Under Conditions of Risk," *Journal of Finance* 19, no. 3 (September 1964): 425–42.

75 **measured trends in American earnings:** Fatih Guvenen, Sam Schulhofer-Wohl, Jae Song, and Motohiro Yogo, "Worker Betas: Five Facts About Systematic Earnings Risk," *American Economic Review* 107, no. 5 (May 2017): 398–403.

76 **tight job market:** Craig Copeland, "Employee Tenure Trends: 1983–2016," *Employee Benefit Research Institute Notes* 38, no. 9 (September 20, 2017), https://www.ebri.org/publications/notes/index.cfm?fa=notesDisp&content_id=3497.

CHAPTER 6: PROSPECT THEORY

82 **"were off the hook":** Phil Hellmuth, *Poker Brat: Phil Hellmuth's Autobiography* (East Sussex, England: D&B Publishing, 2017), 248.

89 **Richard Thaler and Eric Johnson:** Richard Thaler and Eric Johnson, "Gambling with the House Money and Trying to Break Even: The Effects of Prior Outcomes on Risky Choice," *Management Science* 36, no. 6 (June 1990): 643–60.

90 **Economists at Pomona College:** Gary Smith, Michael Levere, and Robert Kurtzman, "Poker Player Behavior After Big Wins and Big Losses," *Management Science* 55, no. 9 (September 2009): 1547–55.

90 **A later study:** David Eil and Jaimie W. Lien, "Staying Ahead and Getting Even: Risk Attitudes of Experienced Poker Players," *Games and Economic Behavior* 87 (September 2014): 50–69.

91 **a morning gain:** Joshua D. Coval and Tyler Shumway, "Do Behavioral Biases Affect Prices?" *Journal of Finance* 60, no. 1 (February 2005): 1–34.

91 **than a loser:** Nicholas Barberis and Wei Xiong, "What Drives the Disposition Effect? An Analysis of a Long-Standing Preference-Based Explanation," *Journal of Finance* 64, no. 2 (April 2009): 751–84, July 2006.

91 **to loss avoidance:** John List, "Does Market Experience Eliminate Market Anomalies?," *Quarterly Journal of Economics* 118, no. 1 (February 2003): 41–71.

CHAPTER 7: RISK MISPERCEPTION

99 **about $7 million:** Barry Meier, "Crazy Eddie's Insane Odyssey," *New York Times,* July 19, 1992, https://www.nytimes.com/1992/07/19/business/crazy-eddie-s-insane-odyssey.html.

100 **more than $60 million:** Meier.

100 **actually lost millions:** Meier.

101 **more than $65 million:** Stephen Labaton, "S.E.C. Files Fraud Case on Retailer," *New York Times,* September 7, 1989, https://www.nytimes.com/1989/09/07/business/sec-files-fraud-case-on-retailer.html.

102 **1,600 additional traffic deaths:** Gerd Gigerenzer, "Dread Risk, September 11, and Fatal Traffic Accidents," *Psychological Science* 15, no. 4 (April 2004): 286–87.

104 **Sociologists surveyed 1,354 teenagers:** Thomas A. Loughran, Greg Pogarsky, Alex R. Piquero, and Raymond Paternoster, "Re-examining the Functional Form of the Certainty Effect in Deterrence Theory," *Justice Quarterly* 29, no. 5 (2012): 712–41.

104 **exercise in power:** Paul Slovic, "Trust, Emotion, Sex, Politics, and Science: Surveying the Risk-Assessment Battlefield," *Risk Analysis* 19, no. 4 (August 1999): 689–701.

105 **deter much crime:** Justin McCrary and Aaron Chalfin, "Criminal Deterrence: A Review of the Literature," *Journal of Economic Literature* 55, no. 1 (March 2017): 5–48.

105 **effective crime deterrent:** Jonathan Klick and Alexander T. Tabarrok, "Using Terror Alert Levels to Estimate the Effect of Police on Crime," *Journal of Law and Economics* 48, no. 1 (April 2005): 267–79.

106 **can also be effective:** Brendan O'Flaherty, *The Economics of Race in the United States* (Cambridge, MA: Harvard University Press, 2015), 362–66.

106 **third-generation pills:** Gerd Gigerenzer, "Making Sense of Health Statistics," *Bulletin of the World Health Organization* 87, no. 8 (August 2009): 567.

107 **people may not understand probabilities:** Gerd Gigerenzer, *Reckoning with Risk: Learning to Live with Uncertainty* (New York: Penguin Books, 2002).

CHAPTER 8: DIVERSIFICATION

116 **earnings at the racetrack:** Jill Stowe and Emily Plant, "Is Moneyball Relevant on the Racetrack? A New Approach to Evaluating Future Racehorses," *Journal of Sports Economics,* http://journals.sagepub.com/doi/full/10.1177/1527002518777977.

117 **twenty thousand Thoroughbred foals:** Jockey Club *Foal Crop* 2018n, http://www.jockeyclub.com/default.asp?section=FB&area=2.

117 **explained by parentage:** Devie Poerwanto and Jill Stowe, "The Relationship Between Sire Representation and Average Yearling Prices in the Thoroughbred Industry," *Journal of Agribusiness* 28, no. 1 (Spring 2010): 61–74.

118 **horse "speed gene":** E. W. Hill, J. Gu, S. S. Eivers, R. G. Fonseca, B. A. McGivney, P. Govindarajan, et al. "A Sequence Polymorphism in *MSTN* Predicts Sprinting Ability and Racing Stamina in Thoroughbred Horses," *PLoS ONE* 5, no. 1 (January 2010): e8645.

119 **in the last forty years:** M. M. Binns et al., "Inbreeding in the Thoroughbred Horse," *Animal Genetics* 43, no. 3 (June 2012): 340–42.

120 **"the average Thoroughbred":** From interview with Binns.

120 **stud fee was $500,000:** Terry Conway, "Northern Dancer: The Patriarch Stallion," America's Best Racing, September 18, 2017, www.americasbestracing.net/the-sport/2017-northern-dancer-the-patriarch-stallion.

120 **Northern Dancer was present:** From an unpublished study by David L. Dink.

121 **Northern Dancer's sprint gene:** Mim A. Bower et al., "The Genetic Origin and History of Speed in the Thoroughbred Racehorse," *Nature Communications* 3 (2012): article number 643.

121 **stayed flat until recently:** Patrick Sharman and Alastair J. Wilson, "Racehorses Are Getting Faster," *Biology Letters* 11, no. 6 (June 2015): 1–5.

122 **less genetic innovation:** Mark W. Denny, "Limits to Running Speed in Dogs, Horses and Humans," *Journal of Experimental Biology* 211 (December 2008): 3836–49.

124 **nearly half do:** Estimated from data from the Federal Reserve Board's 2016 Survey of Consumer Finances, https://www.federalreserve.gov/econres/scfindex.htm.

124 **risk as well as return:** Peter Bernstein, *Capital Ideas: The Improbable Origins of Modern Wall Street* (Hoboken, NJ: John Wiley & Sons, 2005), 57.

126 **risk and fees:** Eugene Fama and Kenneth French, "Luck Versus Skill in the Cross-Section of Mutual Fund Returns," *Journal of Finance* 65, no. 5 (October 2010): 1915–47.

128 **race winner like Gun Runner:** From interviews with Dr. Lambert.

129 **smarter breeding choices:** Based on interviews with Rogers.

129 **genetics has the potential:** Based on interviews with Hill.

CHAPTER 9: DE-RISKING

136 **midwestern corporate executive:** Tony Munoz, "Arnold Donald, President & CEO, Carnival Corporation & plc," *Maritime Executive,* January/February 2017, https://www.maritime-executive.com/magazine/arnold-donald-president--ceo-carnival-corporation-plc.

136 **"sales were at":** Aliya Ram, "Arnold Donald: 'It Stopped Working Because the World Changed,'" *Financial Times,* January 8, 2017, https://www.ft.com/content/3201e790-9abd-11e6-b8c6-568a43813464.

137 chairman until 2005: Heather Cole, "Arnold Donald's Sweet Deal," *St. Louis Business Journal,* May 13, 2004, https://www.bizjournals.com/stlouis/stories/2004/05/17/story1.html.

138 colleagues from Monsanto were surprised: Ram, "Arnold Donald."

143 "The absolute transformation": Jon Pareles, "David Bowie, 21st Century Entrepreneur," *New York Times,* June 9, 2002.

144 Bowie quickly asked: From interview with Pullman.

147 John Padgett from Disney: Chabeli Herrera, "How Carnival Revolutionized Its Guest Experience with Super-Smart Tech," *Miami Herald,* January 8, 2017, www.miamiherald.com/news/business/tourism-cruises/article125317259.html.

147 and his team: Allison Schrager, "Can Carnival Possibly Make a Cruise with Thousands of Passengers Feel Personable?" *Quartz,* April 18, 2018, https://qz.com/1194838/carnival-ocean-medallion-a-disney-magicband-for-cruises/.

CHAPTER 10: INSURANCE

157 Fischer Black and Myron Scholes: Fischer Black, Myron Scholes, "The Pricing of Options and Corporate Liabilities," *Journal of Political Economy* 81, no. 3 (May/June 1973): 637–54.

157 an option's price: Robert Merton, "Theory of Rational Option Pricing," *Bell Journal of Economics and Management Science* 4, no. 1 (Spring 1973): 141–83.

158 20,000 contracts: See "A Brief History of Options," Ally Invest Options Playbook, www.optionsplaybook.com/options-introduction/stock-option-history.

158 4 million options contracts: Chicago Board Options Exchange, *Annual Market Statistics,* http://www.cboe.com/data/historical-options-data/annual-market-statistics.

161 than it prevented: Michael Mueller-Smith, "The Criminal and Labor Market Impacts of Incarceration" (unpublished working paper, 2015), https://sites.lsa.umich.edu/mgms/wp-content/uploads/sites/283/2015/09/incar.pdf.

CHAPTER 11: MORAL HAZARDS

170 "form of nightmares": Greg Long, "Greg Long Recounts Almost Drowning," *Surfing Magazine,* October 1, 2014, https://www.surfer.com/surfing-magazine-archive/surfing-video/greg-long-drowning/.

172 Merton enabled the widespread: Family history and discovery of jet skis as a safety advice from interviews with Brian Keaulana.

175 economist Sam Peltzman: Sam Peltzman, "The Effects of Automobile Safety Regulation," *Journal of Political Economy* 83, no. 4 (August 1975): 677–726.

176 20 percent in 1997: The President's Working Group on Financial Markets, "Hedge Funds, Leverage, and the Lessons of Long-Term Capital Management," April 1999, https://www.treasury.gov/resource-center/fin-mkts/Documents/hedgfund.pdf.

179 finance new technology: William N. Goetzmann, *Money Changes Everything: How Finance Made Civilization Possible* (Princeton, NJ: Princeton University Press, 2017).

180 the trend reversed: National Highway Traffic Safety Administration, "Summary of Motor Vehicle Crashes," August 2018, DOT HS 812 580.

RULE 5: UNCERTAINTY HAPPENS

183 the Knightian uncertainty: Frank Knight, *Risk, Uncertainty, and Profit* (Boston: Houghton Mifflin Co., 1921).

CHAPTER 12: UNCERTAINTY

187 "uniforms and boots": H. R. McMaster, "Battle of 73 Easting" (manuscript available at the Donovan Research Library, Fort Benning, GA): 8, www.benning.army.mil/library/content/Virtual/Donovanpapers/other/73Easting.pdf.

189 "we had practiced": McMaster, 12–13.

190 "until they surrendered": McMaster, 20–21.

190 McMaster told me: From interview with McMaster.

190 "fog of war": Peter Grier, "Preparing for 21st Century Information War," *Government Executive* 8, no. 27 (August 1995): 130. Williamson Murray, "Clausewitz Out, Computer In: Military

Culture and Technological Hubris," *National Interest,* June 1, 1997, https://www.clausewitz
.com/readings/Clause&Computers.htm.

193 **minimizing downside risk:** Colonel Arthur F. Lykke Jr., "Defining Military Strategy," *Military Review* 69, no. 5 (May 1989): 2–8.

193 **Clausewitz identified several factors:** Carl von Clausewitz, *On War,* ed. and trans. Michael Howard and Peter Paret (1976; repr., Princeton, NJ: Princeton University Press, 1989).

195 **"the last conflict":** Williamson Murray, "Thinking About Innovation," *Naval War College Review* 54, no. 2 (Spring 2001): 122–23.

196 **"ponderous English":** Meir Finkel, *On Flexibility: Recovery from Technological and Doctrinal Surprise on the Battlefield* (Stanford, CA: Stanford Security Studies, 2011), 206.

197 ***"the initial surprise":*** Finkel, 2. Italics in the original.

197 **The principles:** Finkel, 1–17.

Index